Women and equal pay

The effects of legislation on female employment and wages in Britain

Women and equal pay

*The effects of legislation on
female employment and wages
in Britain*

A. ZABALZA
Professor of Economics, University of Valencia

and

Z. TZANNATOS
Lecturer in Economics, University of Buckingham

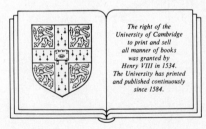

The right of the
University of Cambridge
to print and sell
all manner of books
was granted by
Henry VIII in 1534.
The University has printed
and published continuously
since 1584.

CAMBRIDGE UNIVERSITY PRESS

Cambridge
London   New York   New Rochelle
Melbourne   Sydney

Published by the Press Syndicate of the University of Cambridge
The Pitt Building, Trumpington Street, Cambridge CB2 1RP
32 East 57th Street, New York, NY 10022, USA
10 Stamford Road, Oakleigh, Melbourne 3166, Australia

First published 1985

Printed in Great Britain at the University Press, Cambridge

British Library cataloguing in publication data

Zabalza, Antoni
Women and equal pay: the effects of legislation
on female employment and wages in Britain.
1. Great Britain. Equal Pay Act 1970   2. Wages –
Women – Great Britain
I. Title   II. Tzannatos, Z.
331.4'21'0941   HD6061.2.G7

Library of Congress cataloguing in publication data

Zabalza, Antoni, 1946–
Women and equal pay.
Includes index.
1. Wages – Women – Great Britain.   2. Sex
discrimination in employment – Great Britain.
3. Women – Employment – Law and legislation – Great Britain.
I. Tzannatos, A.   II. Title.
HD6061.2.G7Z33 1985   331.4'2941   85–9681

ISBN 0 521 30188 2

AN

Contents

Foreword

RICHARD LAYARD

When the anti-sex-discrimination legislation was introduced in Britain in the early 1970s, few people were very optimistic about the effects of the legislation. Many believed that the labour market would find ways of avoiding the constraints. In fact, some early studies on the effects of the legislation attributed the taking-off of female wages in the early and mid-1970s to the egalitarian provisions of the incomes policies of the time. However the authors of this book show conclusively that the factor responsible for the increase in female relative wages in the last decade or so was almost exclusively the anti-discrimination legislation. Incomes policies are found to have had a small and, more importantly, a short-lived effect. Today, almost ten years after the legislation was fully implemented, female relative wages are as high as they were in 1976 and this is true for both manual and non-manual as well as full-time and part-time workers. This should not be as surprising as it may appear. The authors show convincingly that the system of determining female wages in an occupation as 'x per cent of male wages' was demolished easily at a stroke of the pen and left little room for non-compliance.

However, their analysis does not end at establishing the actual effects of legislation but goes beyond this to establish also what the *potential* effects of legislation ought to have been. This is a difficult exercise but worth attempting. They conclude that the legislation narrowed that part of the wage gap which is unexplained by differences in economic characteristics by roughly 30 to 50 per cent. Hence, the authors are correct in answering the question, whether women in Britain have benefited from this legislation, with a qualified 'yes', though they both agree that better days for women are still to come.

The study was undertaken at the Centre for Labour Economics at London School of Economics and we are pleased that the authors have produced such a comprehensive and definitive book.

Acknowledgements

The analysis contained in this book was carried out at the Centre for Labour Economics, London School of Economics. We have benefited from comments and suggestions from many people who have read preliminary versions of this work. We would like to thank in particular, P. Allin, M. Arellano, F. Blau, A. Bowey, D. Capron, U. Colombino, G. Chowdhury, J. Ermisch, M. Franklin, J. Garcia, H. Joshi, R. Layard, J. Mincer, J. Muellbauer, W. Narendranathan, S. Nickell, G. Psacharopoulos, N. Rau, A. Robinson, and participants in seminars at the Universities of Warwick and Hull and at the London School of Economics, where parts of this research were presented. Special thanks are due to J.L. Arrufat who, with A. Zabalza, is the joint author of Chapter 5 of this book, to L. Llorens for able research assistance, to B. Jory, P. Pearse and P. Gamble, who superbly typed the many versions of this book and to the Economic and Social Research Council for financial support. Responsibility for the views expressed here rests entirely with the authors.

1

Have women in Britain benefited from equal pay?

e analysis contained in this book suggests that women in Britain have
deed benefited from equal pay legislation. During the seventies they have
'n their relative pay increased by 15 per cent. This improvement cannot
attributed to shifts in female employment from low to high paying
ors of the economy, but is the result of genuine increases in relative
within sectors. It cannot be explained by incomes policies, which have
a much smaller and short lived effect. It has not been achieved at the
nse of female employment, since during this period hours worked by
en have increased by almost 18 per cent relative to hours worked by
Our analysis suggests that the main factor behind this remarkable
se in female pay has been the anti-discriminatory legislation passed
ritain during the seventies.

Why has this type of legislation worked in this country, but failed in
other places? Although there is no complete agreement on this, the results
of equivalent legislation in the United States appear to have been much
less satisfactory and clear cut than in Britain.[1] We have not been able to
analyse the reasons for this difference in detail, but we presume that the
centralised nature of the method of pay determination in Britain may have
had something to do with it. An explicit channel through which the
legislation sought to implement equal pay was the removal of differentiated
female rates in the wage structure of collective agreements and wage
orders, and this was promptly and thoroughly achieved. There is also
evidence that the increase in rates translated quite quickly into increases
in actual pay, and that this did not result in reduction in female
employment.

Has the legislation exerted its full effect? This is a difficult question
because its answer depends crucially on the extent of discrimination that
may exist. We feel that we have been able to show that the male–female

wage differential attributable to discrimination in Britain is less
previously thought, but there is little else we can say without entering
value judgements as to what constitutes discrimination. On the posi
side, we have found that there is a strong association between different
in pay and the extent of non-participation in the market by marr
women. Also, there is evidence that most of the gain achieved by
legislation was completed by 1975, and we have not been able to ident
any further effects. So we suspect that future improvements in relat
pay may be more difficult to achieve.

In the next four chapters of this book we set out in detail the analy
that has led us to these general results. Here, in this chapter, we want
present, in a non-technical fashion, the main components of the argume
and to discuss in some detail the conclusions obtained.

1.1 The facts

The principal facts that we have attempted to explain in this report
shown in Chart 1.1, where we plot relative pay from 1950 to 19
Relative pay is defined as relative hourly earnings of all (full and part-ti
manual and non-manual employees, and its exact calculation and so
are given in the Annex to Chapter 4.[2] The evolution of relative pay sl
in this chart can be divided into three clearly differentiated periods.
a twenty-year period of stability with a very mild downward trend, that
lowered female relative wages from 0.596 in 1950 to 0.580 in 1970 (an
overall 2.7 per cent fall). Then a period of seven years in which relative
pay rose dramatically from 0.580 in 1970 to 0.685 in 1977 (an overall
18.1 per cent increase). Finally a last period in which relative pay appears
to have stabilised itself around the level reached in 1975. In 1980, the last
year used in the econometric analysis of Chapter 4, relative pay was 14.8
per cent higher than in 1970, and the improvement is clearly holding out.
The latest information we have put relative pay in 1983 at 0.665, a 14.7
per cent increase with respect to 1970.

It is certainly tempting to attribute this increase to the anti-
discriminatory legislation enacted in Britain during the seventies. The
Equal Pay Act, requiring equal pay for equivalent work by men and
women, was passed in 1970 but its full implementation was delayed until
the end of 1975 to allow employers time to adjust to the new set of
conditions on pay. The end of 1975 was also the time at which the Sex

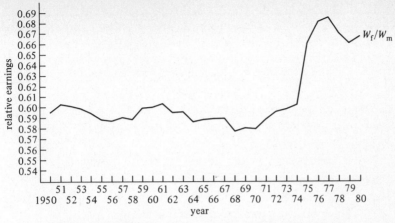

Chart 1.1 Relative hourly earnings in Great Britain (*source*: Annex to Chapter 4)

Discrimination Act, requiring equal employment opportunities for men and women, became law (see Annex to Chapter 1 for a description of these two pieces of legislation). Thus there exists a very clear coincidence between the increase in relative pay and the application of this legislation. But during parts of this period, incomes policies with flat rate provisions were also in force, so they must be taken into account since they could also have contributed to the observed relative wage increase.

However, what happened to employment? Did employers respond to this huge rise in the cost of one type of labour by hiring less of it? Chart 1.2 suggests that nothing of the sort occurred. If we look at the number of women relative to the number of men (*F/M*) employed in the whole economy, we see that the rising trend that was already in evidence before 1970, has persisted during the last ten years. If anything, during this decade women have entered the labour market at a higher rate than before; the rate of growth of female relative employment from 1950 to 1970 was 1.1 per cent per annum, while from 1970 the 1980 it was 1.7 per cent per annum. And the rising tendency does not show any signs of weakening up to 1983, the last year for which we now have information.

We know that parallel to the expansion of female participation, there has been a substantial growth in the part-time employment opportunities offered to women in the labour market. So it is important, in order to make male and female labour more comparable, to take into account the

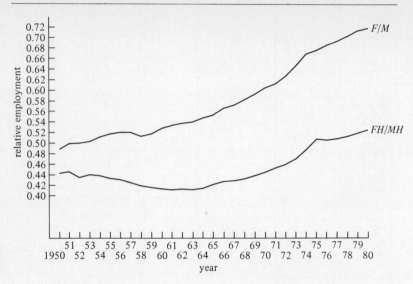

Chart 1.2 Relative employment and man-hours worked in the whole economy (*source*: Annex to Chapter 4)

number of hours worked. The second variable (*FH/MH*) shown in Chart 1.2 is defined as weekly woman-hours over weekly man-hours, and it shows quite unambiguously that part-time work represents an important component of total work by female employees. A graphical measure of the extent of female part-time work is given by the gap between the two plots in Chart 1.2, which has clearly widened steadily during the period considered.

However, even after taking part-time work into account, it cannot be concluded that female work has fallen. Relative to men's, the number of hours worked by women has increased by 17.6 per cent between 1970 and 1980, which represents an average annual rate of growth of 1.6 per cent, and the tendency appears to have been accentuated up to 1983, the latest year for which we now have information. In that year relative employment was 0.561 as compared to 0.523 in 1980. However, during this period there is a noticeable change in the evolution of this variable. Between 1970 and 1975 it grew at an average annual rate of 2.7 per cent, and between 1975 and 1980 at a rate of only 0.6 per cent. This suggests that there has been a certain amount of employment adjustments on the part of employers, and it would be surprising if no such effects had taken place at all. But it is remarkable that relative female employment

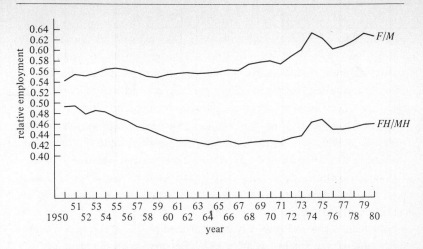

Chart 1.3 Relative employment and man-hours in the private sector (*source*: Annex to Chapter 4)

continued to grow, even after the substantial increases in the relative cost of female labour documented above.

The plots in Chart 1.2 refer to the economy as a whole. So it could be argued that the absence of strong employment adjustments is due to the fact that an important employer of female labour is the public sector, and public employers are not as cost conscious as their private sector homologues. In Chart 1.3 we plot again the variables of the previous chart, but this time excluding mining, transport, utilities (gas, electricity and water), professional and scientific services and public administration, all of these being industries in which public employers are heavily represented. The resulting variables therefore, although not strictly exact, pick up reasonably well the evolution of female relative employment in the private sector during the period considered. They indeed confirm the presumption that a substantial part of the rise in female work is due to the expansion of public sector employment, but it is still true that female relative employment has not experienced any drastic fall. In fact the man-hours variable shows that after a mild but persistent fall in the period 1950 to 1970, the trend is reversed in the last decade with a 7.7 per cent increase in relative employment between 1970 and 1980 (equivalent to an average rate of growth of 0.7 per cent per annum). As with the data for the whole economy, there is a change after 1975, with relative employment going from a rate of growth of 1.9 per cent per annum during the period 1970 to 1975, to a rate of *decline* of 0.4 per cent per annum during the period 1975 to 1980. The fall, however, is not as large as the substantial rise in relative wages would seem to justify, and the preliminary information now available for later years suggests the reappearance of the increasing trend initiated at the beginning of the decade.

So, we have on the one hand a dramatic increase in female relative pay, which coincides both with the period over which the anti-discriminatory legislation was being applied, and with income policies which, due to their flat rate provisions, could also have contributed to the observed rise in pay. On the other hand, we have a fairly steady rise in female relative work, even after taking into account the substantial upsurge of part-time employment. The rise is mostly concentrated in the public sector, and it has been checked somewhat after 1975. But neither in the economy as a whole, nor in the private sector, has the rise in female relative pay resulted in any important fall in the relative amount of hours they have been able to work.

Before entering into an explanation of these facts, it is important to understand the actual manner in which the average female relative wage has increased. Has this been the result of movements of female workers from low to high paying sectors, or of actual rises in relative pay within these sectors? So we turn next to the results we have obtained in Chapter 2, where we have decomposed this average rise of relative pay into its several components.

1.2 Dissecting the average rise in female relative pay

The average rise of female relative pay can be decomposed into three components. A first component that measures by how much relative pay would have increased if relative wages within sectors, and the relative position of sectors, had remained the same, but the distribution of female labour across sectors had changed over time. A second component that measures by how much relative pay would have increased if the relative position of sectors and the distribution of female labour across them had remained constant, but relative wages within sectors had increased. Finally, a third component that measures by how much relative pay would have increased if the distribution of female labour across sectors and relative wages within sectors had remained the same, but the relative position of sectors in the economy had changed. It is important to identify these components because the rise in relative pay could have been due to compositional effects (the first and third components) with women still being paid the same relative to men in each sector. If this had been the case, we would certainly not qualify the operation of the Equal Pay Act as a success, whatever the size of the ensuing increase in pay.

We show in Chapter 2 that the improvement in female relative pay is not due to compositional effects. Whether one takes industries or occupations as the relevant sectors on which to base the decomposition, the result is the same. By far the major factor behind the improvement is an increase in relative pay within industries and within occupations, and this is the case for both contracting and expanding sectors. Also, the timing of this improvement is very similar in all industries and occupations, which suggests that it is more the result of a common cause than the consequence of the particular fortunes of each of the sectors considered.

Another piece of corroborative evidence is given by the evolution of relative pay in public administration. This industrial division is, among those considered, the only one for which relative pay within the sector did not increase during the period 1970 to 1980, and this is consistent with the fact that for the majority of workers in this sector (i.e. non-manual employees), the principle of equal pay was already in force by the beginning of the decade.

Female relative pay within industries and occupations has therefore increased, but is this enough to conclude that female welfare is higher now than before? If the degree of segregation is sufficiently high, one way of achieving equal pay could have been to reduce the pay of male workers in those sectors in which female employment is relatively important. This would result in an increase in the overall female relative pay, and yet it would again be difficult to claim any success for the legislation. We could see whether anything like this has occurred by looking at the industrial and occupational decomposition commented on above, but the groups that we can identify on the basis of collective agreements data are more homogeneous, so it seemed to us worthwhile to repeat the exercise in Chapter 3 with this new division, and also to look more closely at the role that the machinery of pay determination in Britain may have had in the implementation of this legislation.

1.3 The role of centralised pay determination

Overall, our analysis in Chapter 3 does not support the hypothesis that the increase in female relative pay was achieved by lowering men's rather than raising women's pay. For instance, between 1972 and 1980 non-manual workers covered by wages boards, with 67 per cent female employment, and the collective agreement for ancillary workers in the National Health Service, which has a 61 per cent proportion of female employment, both experienced a substantial increase in female relative pay within the agreement, and no deterioration in the relative position of men's pay. Only male teachers seem to have suffered a deterioration in their relative position since 1972, but they belong to an agreement in which equal pay was already in force since 1961, so it can hardly be the case that this was due to the manner in which the legislation was being implemented.

The data on collective agreements can also be used to understand the channels through which the anti-discriminatory legislation has operated. The system of pay determination in Britain is fairly centralised. A relatively small number of collective agreements determine the rates of pay of a very large number of workers. It is therefore conceivable that the system of collective agreements has played an important role in implementing the anti-discriminatory legislation, particularly when taking into account that the Equal Pay Act explicitly singles out the elimination of differential wage rates for women in the salary structures determined by collective agreements and wage orders. Unions' and employers' representatives will have certainly found it very difficult to ignore the pressure imposed by the legislation on the equalisation of wage rates, and this is what the data indicate.

Already in 1971, the first year of the adjustment period, there was a noticeable effect on relative *rates* of pay for manual employees, which during the previous twenty years had remained particularly stable. The effect gathered pace quite quickly, to culminate in 1976 with full equality in male and female rates of pay. This is what happened to rates of pay. What happened to the actual wages paid to these workers is more difficult to know because we do not have the necessary information for all the years and for the whole of the manual covered sector. But it is evident that overall relative earnings (for both covered and non-covered manual workers) followed suit quite quickly. So much so, that the relation between earnings and rates was hardly disturbed away from its long-run trend as a result of this equalisation in the wage rate structures.

We would have liked to identify separately what has happened to covered and uncovered relative earnings over time, and to consider both manual and non-manual workers. This would have allowed us to check whether the main and first thrust of the legislation took place among covered workers, and whether from there it spread out to the uncovered sector. This, however, was not possible due to lack of data, and we had to content ourselves with the comparison done by Gregory and Thomson (1981) for the years 1973 and 1978. The latter year is probably too late to discern any significant difference between covered and uncovered sectors since, as we will see below, by that time most of the effect of the legislation had already been exerted. There may have been a point in time in which the increase in relative pay among covered workers was leading that of uncovered workers, but the Gregory and Thomson data (presented in Table 3.2) show quite clearly that by 1978 this lead had already disappeared, and that the rise in relative pay was quite general. In fact, by 1978 the rise in relative pay of non-manual female workers was larger in the non-covered than in the covered sector; and even among manual workers, the difference in favour of the covered sector was not very large.

So we conclude from this analysis that there is evidence that collective agreements started to move towards equalisation quite early in the decade, that these increases in relative rates resulted in corresponding and contemporaneous increases in relative earnings, and that the effect on average earnings was not confined to the covered sector but also spilled over to non-covered employees.

All this amounts, in our opinion, to a fairly impressive body of evidence in favour of the effectiveness of anti-discriminatory legislation. But so far we have not considered any factor, other than this legislation, that may have also influenced relative pay. Autonomous shifts in female labour supply, changes in the industrial structure, or other government policies could also have had an impact on the relative position of female workers. Thus, we need to consider the labour market as a whole, taking into account not only relative employment but also other forces that, through their effect on demand and supply, may have helped relative pay to rise.

1.4 The impact of anti-discriminatory legislation on relative pay

In Chapter 4 we have considered the simultaneous effect that these other forces may have had on relative pay. We have found that even after taking into account the concomitant change of other variables, together with their interrelation within the labour market, anti-discriminatory legislation has had a positive and significant effect on both relative earnings and relative employment of women. Neither the level of economic activity, nor incomes policies, nor changes in the industrial structure, nor changes in labour supply conditions, can explain, in isolation or jointly considered, the remarkable increase that female relative pay has experienced during the seventies.

So then, how has the legislation operated to achieve this result? Our econometric analysis suggests that it has operated by raising the demand for female labour relative to male labour and, on the basis of the issues discussed above, our preferred interpretation to justify this change in behaviour is the following. As a consequence of the anti-discriminatory legislation and its implementation by collective agreements, employers were faced with a higher price for female labour and, on the whole, did not take any drastic action to reduce female employment. This, in the context of the labour market model we have used, is equivalent to an increase in the demand for women relative to men, and this is precisely the effect that our econometric estimates tend to suggest.

We have not attempted to explain why employers did not react otherwise, but the existence of sizeable turnover costs (i.e. fixed expenses related to hiring and firing), the likely deterioration of labour force morale that large employment adjustments would entail, and the possible threat of union reprisals, are all reasons that may be related to their fairly passive acceptance of this legislation. Researchers of this issue in the United States have tended to interpret this increase in demand as a fall in the extent of discrimination by employers, induced by the penalties associated with the legislation. But financial penalties for breaking anti-discriminatory legislation in the United Kingdom are not as important as in the United States, and it is doubtful that they have played an important role in changing employers' behaviour in this country.

We have estimated that the isolated effect of anti-discriminatory legislation has been to increase female relative pay by about 19 per cent, and that this effect took place gradually over the first half of the seventies. This induced an increase in female labour supply, which in turn pushed down relative pay somewhat. In the end both female relative employment and female relative pay were higher than their pre-legislation levels; relative employment by more than 12 per cent and relative pay by about 15 per cent.

The estimated timing of the effects is also interesting. We have found that the effect of the legislation on relative pay was beginning to be felt as early as 1971, which is consistent with the information we have on actions directed at the implementation of equal pay by collective agreements. The main thrust, however, was concentrated in the years 1974 and 1975. It is important to emphasise that these are permanent effects. The gains attributed to incomes policies, on the other hand, are transitory and amount to less than 2 per cent. This explains quite well the shape of the evolution of relative wages in Chart 1.1. From 1970 to 1975 equal pay legislation helps to lift female wages up to around two-thirds of male wages. Then comes the effect of incomes policies causing the bulge observed in the years 1976 and 1977, which quickly disappears due to the temporary nature of these policies. After 1978, with the influence of incomes policies gone, relative pay stabilises itself around the two-thirds level achieved in 1975.

Was the legislation only operative in the public sector? As we have seen above, the evolution of female employment in the private sector has been quite different from that in the public sector, and it could well be that while relative demand for female labour has increased in the public sector, it has gone down in the private. Our results, however, suggest that this is not the case. The substantial increase in relative pay cannot be explained on the basis of the possible non-cost-minimising behaviour of the public sector. Although it is true that, during the period considered, female employment in the public sector expanded at a faster rate than in the private sector, we have not been able to identify any difference of substance between the two sectors as far as the effect of anti-discriminatory legislation is concerned. The isolated effect of the legislation on that sector would have been to increase female relative pay by 19.6 per cent, as compared to 18.8 per cent when the public sector is also included. We have also found a practically identical wage elasticity of the relative demand function and a similar effect from incomes policies.

We have found then that anti-discriminatory legislation has had an effect, and that its impact can be estimated to be around a 19 per cent increase in female relative pay. Is this a big gain? To answer this question we need to compare this 19 per cent gain with the maximum gain that the legislation could have achieved, and to measure this maximum we must find out what is the extent of sex discrimination in the market. This is the object of the last chapter in this book.

1.5 How much discrimination is left?

Our last task has been to measure the extent of market sex discrimination. That is, the differential in wages between men and women that cannot be explained on the basis of differences in productive capacity. We must emphasize from the outset that this is a very restrictive concept of discrimination, for decisions concerning the acquisition of this productive capacity can themselves be affected by discrimination. Also the measurement of productive capacity is in itself a difficult task, and the proxies that are normally used may be poor and largely removed from the concept they are meant to represent. Despite these difficulties, we believe it is worthwhile to attempt this exercise because, in addition to identifying factors that may be related to wage differentials, it offers at least a benchmark on which to measure the effectiveness of anti-discriminatory policies, although the legislation is only designed to eliminate discrimination within the individuals' organisation.

The measurement of sex discrimination in the market proceeds normally along the following lines. We first posit a relationship between the wage that a person can expect to obtain in the market and the amount of productive characteristics that this person holds. By productive characteristics we understand any trait, innate or acquired, which is valued by the market, although the two main items typically considered are education and market experience. Once this relationship is established, we measure how much the market rewards each unit of these characteristics for men and for women. If the rewards per unit of characteristic are the same, then we say that there is no market discrimination. Thus, we could find a situation in which no market discrimination exists and yet wages were higher for men than for women. This would be the case if on average the amount of productive characteristics that men hold is greater than that held by women. In general both the amount of characteristics and the reward of these characteristics may differ between men and women. Then, the measurement of discrimination consists of identifying that part of the wage differential generated solely by the different rewards per unit of characteristic that the market sets, depending on whether the holder of these characteristics is a man or a woman.

With the data normally available to researchers, the measurement of these characteristics is not always an easy task. A case in point is that posed by market experience. The cross-sectional data that we have at our disposal, which is the sort of data normally used, does not give information on the actual number of years of experience, and this has forced researchers to use as a proxy the amount of *potential* market experience; that is, the age of the person minus the age at which he or she left full-time education. This is likely to be a good proxy for men but a very unreliable one for women, many of whom experience significant interruptions in their labour market participation. The problem arises because the estimation of the returns to these characteristics may be affected if we measure them incorrectly. Also, using only potential experience means ignoring the negative effect that breaks in participation may have on expected wages, due to possible depreciation of market skills while staying at home.

In Chapter 5 we have found that these issues are important and that they make a substantial difference to the measurement of sex discrimination. For instance, as measured from the General Household Survey, the average wage of married women relative to that of married men in 1975 was 0.623. That is, married women were earning 38 per cent less than married men. If we had used the concept of *potential* market experience in our analysis, we would conclude that only 15 per cent of this gap could be explained by differences in personal attributes,[3] the rest being attributable to market discrimination. If, on the other hand, we use *actual* market experience (which we have estimated by means of a labour supply model), we would conclude that differences in personal attributes explain more than 21 per cent of the wage gap. Moreover, of the remaining 79 per cent, we are able to identify that a portion as high as 45 per cent is due to interruptions in labour force participation by married women, leaving 34 per cent of the gap unexplained.[4] The reason why now, using *actual* market experience, we are able to attribute a higher percentage of the gap to differences in personal attributes is simple. While there is a small difference in the amount of *potential* experience that men and women hold on the average, the differences in *actual* experience are much more acute. For our sample the average *potential* experience was 24.5 years for men and 23.2 years for women. Using *actual* experience, we still have 24.5 years for men but only 15.9 years for women. Thus using potential experience rather than actual experience tends to make the productive characteristics held by men and women more equal than they actually are.

Probably the most interesting result of this exercise is the strong relationship that we find between low female pay and interruptions in labour force participation. As mentioned above, almost half of the wage gap can be accounted for by this factor. The average woman of our sample who interrupts her participation in the labour market for one year, not only loses the 3.3 per cent increase in wages that she would have obtained during that year, but when returning she starts at a level of wages 2.9 per cent lower than when she left. The question then arises, can this treatment by the market be interpreted as discriminatory? We do not believe we can give a satisfactory answer to this issue. The negative relationship between female pay and home time may be reflecting very different situations. A computer programmer with five years of past market experience who returns to the labour market after a three-year break may find herself both a bit rusty as far as her programming skills are concerned, and quite at a loss among the new technology developed during her absence. It would be unwarranted to conclude that an employer who pays this woman less than a younger male programmer with five years of uninterrupted experience is behaving in a discriminatory fashion. In one case we would have an individual with five years of largely irrelevant experience; in the other, an individual with five years of experience which have kept him abreast of the latest technological developments. We would say that although both individuals have five years of market experience, the woman in question is less productive than her male colleague, and we would not therefore interpret the ensuing pay differential as being discriminatory. But there may be other situations in which technological advances are less dramatic, and (or) in which the skill content of jobs is much lower, where absence from the labour force may have a very insignificant detrimental effect on productive capacity. If in these situations employers use labour market interruptions as a reason to pay women less than otherwise equivalent men, then the differential ought to be termed discriminatory.

Thus it is impossible to say which part of this 45 per cent of the wage gap (which we have associated with interruptions in labour force participation) is discriminatory and which part is not. And because of this ambiguity, it is also impossible to evaluate precisely the extent to which the legislation has exerted or not its full potential effect. If we were to consider the whole of the wage differential due to non-participation as discriminatory, we would conclude that there is still a long way to be covered. *Under this extreme assumption*, the complete elimination of discrimination, as seen from the year 1975, would involve an increase of the relative wage for married women from 0.623 to 0.905. That is, a percentage increase in average relative pay of 45.3 per cent. These results refer to married women only, but since the extent of discrimination between married and single women is not very different once actual participation is taken into account, we can use them as representatives of the whole female population. Now, as we have seen in the previous section, by 1975 most of the effect of the anti-discriminatory legislation had already taken place. So it is reasonable to assume that the above figures, which correspond to the year 1975, already incorporate the gain resulting from this legislation. We have measured this gain, in Chapter 4, to be an 18.8 percentage increase of the average relative pay. Therefore, we have that, as compared with the pre-legislation situation (that is, as compared with 1970), the total potential increase in relative pay needed to eliminate discrimination would be 64.1 per cent. Of this, the legislation has achieved an increase of 18.8 per cent, which represents 29.3 per cent of the total potential increase.

However, if we were to consider that the whole of the wage differential due to non-participation is not discriminatory (that is, that it is justified by the lower productive capacity resulting from depreciation of labour market skills), then the degree of success of the legislation would be much higher. Under this other exteme assumption, the complete elimination of discrimination, as seen from the year 1975, would involve an increase of the relative wage from 0.623 to 0.731. Using the same procedure as above, the total potential increase since 1970 needed to eliminate discrimination would be 36.1 per cent. So, the 18.8 per cent achieved by the legislation would in this case represent 52.1 per cent of the total potential increase.

We have then that under these two extreme assumptions, the legislation would be thought of as having achieved between 30 and 50 per cent of the total possible gains needed to eliminate discrimination completely. The truth is probably somewhere in between, so we have these two figures as the limiting values of the range of possible outcomes.[5]

Thus, we think it is reasonable to answer *yes* to the question posed by the title of this chapter. Anti-discriminatory legislation in Britain has had an effect on female pay, and this effect is probably large relative to the total needed to eliminate discrimination. Even if the legislation had only managed to achieve 30 per cent of the total possible gains, this would be by all standards a remarkable performance for a policy of economic regulation. Our conjecture is that the effect has probably been larger than that. It is also important to realise, in the light of the results obtained here, that even if discriminatory differentials were to be eliminated, men would on average still be paid more than women, mainly because of the larger and more continuous amount of labour market experience they hold. This differential could of course be narrowed down further, but we believe that for this to be achieved other types of changes, making female participation in the labour market easier or more attractive, would need to take place.

2

Male–female differentials in pay and employment: evidence from the New Earnings Survey

The purpose of this chapter is largely descriptive. We would like to go behind the evolution of relative pay and employment depicted in Charts 1.1 and 1.2, and enquire more closely into several aspects of these differentials. To do that we concentrate on the period 1970 to 1980, and we use information from the *New Earnings Survey*. In the first section we consider the evolution of average relative wages and of relative employment over the last decade for manual and non-manual workers, and for full-time and part-time workers. Second, we would like to see whether the rise in relative pay is due to compositional effects or whether it reflects genuine increases in female wages. For purposes of analysis the wage differentials between men and women can be decomposed into two parts: that part due to the different distribution of the female labour force between sectors of the economy, and that part due to the different pay that women receive within each of these sectors or groups. In the second section we consider to what extent the increase in female relative pay has been due to an improvement in the female employment distribution or to an improvement in wages within the existing distribution. The last issue we consider (in the third section) concerns only pay, but rather than looking at averages, we investigate how the whole distribution of pay has evolved over time. The chapter ends with a section in which the main conclusions are summarised.

2.1 Relative pay and employment during the seventies

The last decade has witnessed important changes in the relative pay and employment of women. We leave for a later chapter the analysis of the causes that may lie behind these changes, and concentrate here on their description. This is a useful exercise. It helps not only to organise the data

16

and to perceive more clearly the different dimensions of these changes, but also to suggest explanatory hypotheses. Although these will not be pursued here, we will see that in many cases simply inspection of data takes us some way towards an understanding of the underlying forces.

Possibly the best example is given by the overall evolution of relative pay and employment for full-time workers. Between 1970 and 1980, female relative hourly wages increased by 11.2 per cent, and female relative employment by 12.9 per cent. The increase in relative wages was quite general, affecting both manual workers (an increase of 14.9 per cent) and non-manual workers (an increase of 16.4 per cent). The increase in relative employment, on the other hand, was exclusively due to the expansion of female workers in the non-manual sector. Relative employment in that sector increased by 5.0 per cent during the period, while in the manual sector it decreased by 0.3 per cent. It is interesting that while relative wages in the two sectors had a similar history over the period, the evolution of relative employment was so different. If the evolution of relative employment was due only to output expansion in each sector, we would expect a much smaller increase of relative wages in the manual sector. The fact that this is not the case seems to suggest that other factors may have affected relative wages *and* that these factors exerted a uniform influence on both sectors. That the equal pay legislation enacted during the period was among these factors is of course a strong possibility, but we will need to take into account other variables that may also have changed over the period before this influence can be ascertained.

Table 2.1 and Charts 2.1, 2.2 and 2.3 present the year to year details of this evolution. The most obvious feature of these data is the substantial increase in female relative wages during the period 1973–7. This increase is common to both sectors and the pattern that follows is also very similar: moderate increases in the first and last year (1974 and 1977), and very large increases in the two middle years (1975 and 1976). Does this large increase in relative wages coincide with a parallel increase in output? The literature on wage differentials suggests that gaps tend to narrow during upturns of economic activity (Wachter, 1970). In our case, the first substantial increases in relative wages coincide with falls in the real level of GDP. Between 1973 and 1974 it decreased by 1.4 per cent, and between 1974 and 1975 by 0.9 per cent. Thus it looks as if the jump in relative wages was quite unrelated to the cycle, or at least to the contemporaneous depression. Chiplin *et al.* (1980) suggest that this

Table 2.1. Relative employment and wages of full-time workers 1970—80 (per cent)

Year	Manual workers		Non-manual workers		All workers	
	F/M	W_f/W_m	F/M	W_f/W_m	F/M	W_f/W_m
1970	21.30	61.68	73.91	52.49	40.37	63.68
1971	21.20	61.25	73.18	53.17	40.07	63.28
1972	21.37	61.76	74.52	53.98	40.90	64.02
1973	21.48	62.00	74.23	54.31	41.35	63.66
1974	21.38	64.43	73.27	55.54	41.01	65.11
1975	19.63	68.04	72.53	60.65	40.86	69.87
1976	19.96	71.06	74.92	62.58	42.27	72.59
1977	20.61	71.74	76.36	63.05	43.52	72.90
1978	20.96	71.99	76.03	61.23	44.01	71.31
1979	20.78	70.22	77.71	61.00	44.55	70.50
1980	21.24	70.85	77.60	61.10	45.59	70.82

Notes: (i) 'Year' refers to April of that year.
(ii) 'Employment' refers to all full-time adults in the sample (i.e. men aged 21 and over and women aged 18 and over) whose pay for the survey period was not affected by absence.
(iii) Wages are average gross hourly earnings excluding overtime pay and overtime hours of those adults whose pay was not affected by absence.
Source: *New Earnings Survey*, 1970 to 1980.

increase could be due to the operation of incomes policies, which over the last decade have been explicitly equalising. There are two issues here. First, although the policies were intended to be equalising, the actual results in this direction were very limited (Ashenfelter and Layard, 1979). Second, if the increase was due only to the effects of incomes policies, it is difficult to understand why the level of relative wages has remained so high after 1977. Incomes policies may have had some effect, but clearly there are other factors at work.

The evolution of relative employment is also informative. As commented on above, relative employment in manual occupations practically remained constant over the whole decade, while in non-manual occupations it increased substantially. This suggests that demand effects may be at work here, and is consistent with the presumption that output in non-manufacturing industries with a largely non-manual work force has expanded more than output in manufacturing industries.

So far we have concentrated only on full-time workers, which is the segment of the labour force on which, in principle, the equal pay

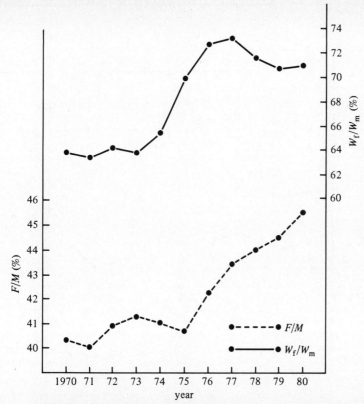

Chart 2.1 Relative (female/male) employment and wages for full-time workers (manual and non-manual)

legislation may have had a more marked effect. Most part-time workers are women who work in segregated jobs, which do not afford an easy comparison with similar tasks performed by men. This is the argument underlying the presumption that the legislation has been ineffective for a large contingent of women engaged in part-time work. The argument does not carry much weight, however. Segregation is also very important among full-time women workers, and yet their relative wages have increased substantially. The possibility of comparisons with men's jobs does not seem therefore to have been a very important factor in explaining compliance with the law. In fact, when we look at data relating to *only* part-time women, we see that the behaviour of their wages relative to those of full-time men is very similar to that discussed above for full-time

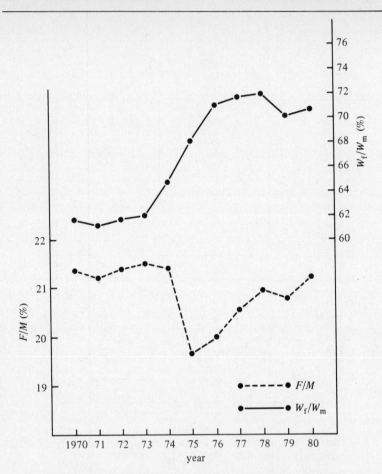

Chart 2.2 Relative (female/male) employment and wages for full-time manual workers

women.[6] Although for part-time women we only have detailed data for the period 1972—9, the most substantial increase in relative wages is again observed for the period 1973—5, also with a very large increase (8.9 per cent) in the year 1975 (see Table 2.2 and Chart 2.4). The overall rate of increase is 12.4 per cent, which is even larger than that of full-time women for the corresponding period. Thus, it is not possible to conclude that the behaviour of relative wages has been different for part-time as opposed to full-time female employees.

It would now be interesting to check whether this wage behaviour is

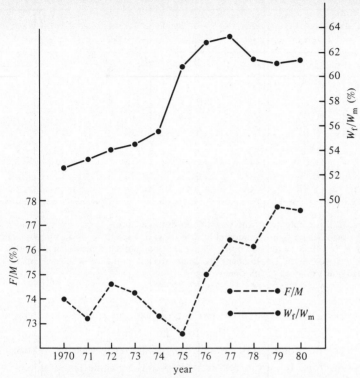

Chart 2.3 Relative (female/male) employment and wages for full-time non-manual workers

uniform across industries, occupations and age groups, and to what extent it is due to actual increases in relative pay within these sectors or just to compositional changes. We turn to this issue in the next section.

2.2 The decomposition of changes in relative pay and employment

Female relative wages could have increased because women are now paid more in all sectors, or because (although paid the same) women have moved into industries or occupations in which relative pay is normally high, or because of a mixture of both reasons. In this section we attempt to disentangle these different aspects of the change by looking at the evolution of relative pay within industries, occupations and age groups.

Table 2.2. Relative employment and wages of part-time women 1972—9 (per cent)

	Manual workers		Non-manual workers		All workers	
Year	F/M	W_f/W_m	F/M	W_f/W_m	F/M	W_f/W_m
1972	10.92	55.99	11.23	44.48	11.03	50.68
1973	9.92	57.45	10.25	44.62	10.04	51.43
1974	10.27	59.93	11.74	44.39	10.82	52.77
1975	9.07	64.26	10.99	49.60	9.84	57.47
1976	10.33	66.03	12.01	50.47	11.01	58.59
1977	10.85	66.30	11.78	51.78	11.23	59.23
1978	10.74	65.68	12.12	49.94	11.32	57.82
1979	11.16	63.65	12.78	49.95	11.84	56.97

Notes: (i) For employment and wages definition, see notes (ii) and (iii) to Table 2.1.
(ii) To make these figures comparable with those in Table 2.1, female employment is given in full-time equivalent units. These are obtained by weighting the number of part-time women in employment by their average hours of work relative to the average hours of work of full-time women.
Source: *New Earnings Survey*, 1972 to 1979.

There exists a substantial amount of segregation between male and female workers and it is therefore important to look at potential improvements coming not so much from better wages in traditionally female sectors, but from redistribution of the female labour force into better paying sectors. Before we actually carry out the decomposition analysis it is instructive to look at the extent to which male and female workers are segregated. Table 2.3 lists, for 1980, occupations in order of female representation beginning with those in which the proportion of females was highest. The first column shows the number of women in the occupation relative to the total number of female workers, the second column shows relative male employment, and the last two columns the corresponding cumulative distributions. The first thing to notice is the much more even distribution of male workers. Women are largely concentrated in three occupations: clerical and related; professional and related in education, welfare and health; and catering, cleaning, hairdressing and other personal services. In fact, 61 per cent of female workers are concentrated in just two broad occupational groups, while it takes five such groups to employ 55 per cent of the male work-force. The second important feature of Table 2.3 is the substantial degree of segregation that

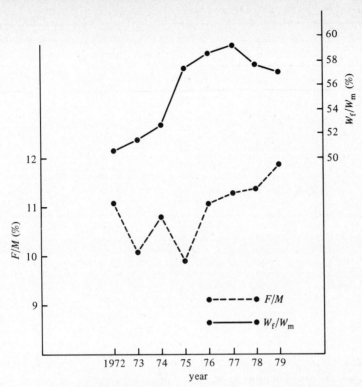

Chart 2.4 Relative employment and wages for part-time women (manual and non-manual)

it shows. Less than 30 per cent of men are in occupations which employ almost 90 per cent of women.

So, given this degree of segregation it might be the case that a significant part of the female wage increase reported above is simply due to a redistribution of the female labour force across sectors, rather than to an improvement of pay within these sectors. To elucidate this question, we define female relative wages as follows:

$$\frac{W_f}{W_m} = \left(\sum_{i=1}^{n} f_i W_{fi} \right) \Big/ W_m$$

$$= \sum_{i=1}^{n} f_i \frac{W_{fi}}{W_{mi}} \frac{W_{mi}}{W_m} \tag{2.1}$$

Table 2.3. *The distribution (%) of female and male employment across occupations (1980)*

Occupation	Female	Male	Female cumulative	Male cumulative
Clerical and related (N)	42.39	8.70	42.39	8.70
Professional (education, welfare, health) (N)	18.48	5.61	60.87	14.31
Catering, cleaning, etc. and other personal service (M)	10.15	3.59	71.02	17.90
Painting, assembling, inspecting, packaging etc. (M)	6.47	4.51	77.49	22.41
Selling (N)	6.14	3.95	83.63	26.36
Making and repairing (ex. metal) (M)	4.17	2.52	87.80	28.88
Professional (management and administration) (N)	2.40	7.18	90.20	36.06
Managerial (ex. general management) (N)	2.35	8.15	92.55	44.21
Processing, making etc. (metal and electrical) (M)	1.80	18.53	94.35	62.74
Processing (ex. metal) (M)	1.80	3.46	96.15	66.20
Professional (science, engineering, technology, etc.) (N)	1.33	8.27	97.48	74.47
Transport, materials, storing and moving (M)	1.04	11.31	98.52	85.78
Literary, artistic and sports (N)	0.50	0.86	99.02	86.64
Security and protective services (N)	0.40	2.52	99.42	89.16
General management (N)	—	—	—	89.16
Farming, fishing and related (M)	—	2.00	—	91.16
Construction, mining and related (M)	—	4.60	—	95.76
Miscellaneous (M)	—	1.67	—	97.43

Notes: (i) N, non-manual; M, manual.
(ii) Occupations 'clerical and related', 'selling' and 'security and protective services' classified as non-manual, include some manual employees.
(iii) Figures relate to full-time adults, whose pay was not affected by absence during the survey period.

or

$$r = \sum_{i=1}^{n} f_i r_i s_i$$

which expresses overall female relative pay ($r = W_f/W_m$) as the product of three separate components. The proportion of women in a given sector (f_i), the relative wage *within* this sector ($r_i = W_{fi}/W_{mi}$) and the position of this sector relative to the average, measured in terms of men's pay ($s_i = W_{mi}/W_m$). Changes over time in the overall relative differential must come from changes over time in each of these three components. If we look at relative changes and indicate these by a dot over the corresponding variable (e.g. $\Delta r/r = \dot{r}$, $\Delta f_i/f_i = \dot{f}_i$, etc.), it is easy to show that

$$\dot{r} = \sum_{i=1}^{n} k_i \dot{f}_i + \sum_{i=1}^{n} k_i \dot{r}_i + \sum_{i=1}^{n} k_i \dot{s}_i + \text{remainder}$$

$$\text{where } k_i = \frac{f_i r_i s_i}{r} \tag{2.2}$$

This expression indicates the isolated effects of (proportional) changes in each of the three components discussed above. The first summation ($\Sigma k_i \dot{f}_i$) measures by how much relative pay would have increased (proportionally) if relative wages within sectors and the relative position of sectors had remained the same ($\dot{r}_i = \dot{s}_i = 0$), but the distribution of female labour across sectors had changed over time. The second ($\Sigma k_i \dot{r}_i$) measures by how much relative pay would have increased due to the change of relative wages within sectors, other factors being the same ($\dot{f}_i = \dot{s}_i = 0$). The third ($\Sigma k_i \dot{s}_i$) measures by how much relative wages would have changed due to the change in the relative position of sectors. For ease of reference we call these components a 'structure effect', a 'differential effect' and a 'sector ranking effect'. So the decomposition in (2.2) can be expressed for mnemonic purposes as

$r =$ structure effect + differential effect + sector ranking effect +

   remainder

If overall pay in sectors in which women are over-represented had improved relative to sectors in which they are under-represented, then the overall female relative wage would have increased even if there was no change in the male–female differential within sectors or in the distribution of female employment. Clearly the first two elements are the most important from our point of view. The equal pay legislation cannot have influenced directly the relative position of occupations s_i, but, if effective, it could have operated through changes in the distribution of female employment f_i (the equal opportunity aspect of the legislation) or through changes in relative pay within sectors r_i (the equal pay aspect of the legislation).[7] Of course, this does not imply that changes in these elements are sufficient (or even necessary) evidence in favour of the effectiveness of this legislation. There are many other factors that may have generated these changes and that will have to be taken into account before a firm answer can be given. The remainder is composed of three second order effects plus one third order effect. They are normally small in magnitude and thus ignored in the following analysis.[8]

The three divisions we will use to evaluate expression (2.2) are industries, occupations and age. Unfortunately the New Earnings Survey does not provide data on employees if the sampled number is less than 100 or on average wages if the standard error of the estimate is greater than 2 per cent of the average. This means that the analysis by industries and occupations is limited to a relatively small number of sectors to avoid empty cells at the initial and final years of comparison. The results, however, are unlikely to be very distorted for two reasons. First, the sectors examined represent a large proportion of female workers (for industries, two-thirds, and for occupations three-quarters in year 1980). Second, when we repeat the analysis only for manual workers (where the number of industries without empty cells is smaller) the conclusions obtained are practically the same.[9]

Table 2.4 presents the decomposition of the proportional change in the wage differential between 1970 and 1980 by industry, and between 1973 and 1980 by occupation. During these periods the female—male wage ratio increased by 11.9 per cent in the eight industrial sectors considered, and by 15.3 per cent in the eight occupations considered (it increased by 11.2 per cent overall, see Table 2.1). The results from the two divisions considered (industries and occupations) are consistent and show very clearly that most of the rate of growth in female relative wages is explained by increases within sectors. Even if the relative standing of industries and occupations had remained the same during the decade, and even if women had not moved from the industries and occupations in which they were originally placed, relative wages in the eight industries considered would have grown by 13.3 per cent, and in the eight occupations by 14.6 per

Table 2.4. *Decomposition of the proportional change in relative (F/M) wages by selected industries (1970–80) and occupations (1973–80)*

Industry	Structure effect $k_i \dot{f_i}$ (1)	Differential effect $k_i \dot{r_i}$ (2)	Industry ranking effect $k_i \dot{s_i}$ (3)
Chemical	−0.651	0.469	−0.091
Electrical	−1.939	1.303	−1.141
Vehicles	−0.704	0.592	−0.175
Transport	0.248	0.143	0.249
Distributive trades	−1.763	2.959	−0.166
Professional	4.432	5.956	−3.872
Miscellaneous	0.966	2.042	0.307
Public admin.	1.098	−0.129	1.666

$\dot{r} = 11.923$ $\qquad \Sigma k_i \dot{f_i} = 1.687 \; \Sigma k_i \dot{r_i} = 13.335 \; \Sigma k_i \dot{s_i} = -2.223$

Occupation	Structure effect $k_i \dot{f_i}$ (4)	Differential effect $k_i \dot{r_i}$ (5)	Occupation ranking effect $k_i \dot{s_i}$ (6)
Clerical and related	5.736	7.276	−0.514
Selling	0.133	1.377	−0.048
Personal service	−0.659	1.695	0.712
Processing (ex. metal)	−0.906	0.928	0.046
Making, repairing (ex. metal)	−1.541	1.096	−0.239
Metal processing, etc.	−1.122	0.509	−0.011
Painting, assembling, etc.	−0.386	1.542	−0.229
Transport, moving, storing, etc.	−0.121	0.209	0.046

$\dot{r} = 15.297$ $\qquad \Sigma k_i \dot{f_i} = 1.334 \; \Sigma k_i \dot{r_i} = 14.632 \; \Sigma k_i \dot{s_i} = -0.237$

Notes: (i) For the actual decomposition formula, see equation (2.2).
(ii) $\dot{f_i}$ relates to all full-time adults whose pay was not affected by absence; $\dot{r_i}$ and $\dot{s_i}$ to average gross hourly earnings excluding overtime effects.
Source: *New Earnings Survey*, 1970, 1973, 1980.

cent. The distribution of female workers between sectors changed somewhat, and towards sectors where pay was higher, but the overall contribution to the rate of change of the relative wage was smaller than that of pay increases within sectors. Also of minor importance was the influence of alterations in the relative importance of sectors in terms of men's pay.

Since occupations are much narrower categories in terms of type of job performed, it is convenient to concentrate on the decomposition by occupations to see what went on behind these overall effects. Looking at changes in relative pay within sectors (column 5) we see that this went up over the decade in all eight occupations, but by far the occupation that contributed most was 'clerical and related'. Even if nothing else had changed, increases in relative pay within this occupation would have raised the overall relative pay of women by 7.3 per cent between 1973 and 1980. The increase in the proportion of women working in this occupational category was also an important factor. In fact, 'clerical and related' is one of the only two occupations (the other is 'selling') which experienced a gain the employment distribution illustrating the considerable shift in female employment from manual to non-manual jobs. What is striking is that no matter whether one occupation expanded or contracted in terms of female employment, relative pay always increased.

It is interesting to note, before leaving Table 2.4, the decomposition results for 'public administration' in the industrial division. It is the only sector for which relative pay within the industry did not increase during the period, and this is consistent with the fact that for the majority of workers in this sector (i.e. non-manual employees) the principle of equal pay was already in force by the beginning of the decade.

Table 2.5 shows how these changes occurred through time. Each row indicates the contribution of the three summation terms of (2.2) to the year to year percentage increase in relative pay. Concentrating on the occupational division (the results are very similar when using the industrial division) we see that the largest effect during almost all years was that due to changes in relative wages within occupations. Compositional effects due to the redistribution of the female labour force were very small in all years, and only in the years 1975–6 and 1978–9 were effects due to realignments of overall pay between occupations important. Within the period considered, only in one year (1978–9) did women's relative pay fall significantly and this can be attributed more to a general worsening of

Table 2.5. *Decomposition of the year-to-year proportional change in the wage differential by industries (1970–80) and occupation (1973–80)*

	By industries			
Year	Total change $\dot{r}$	Structure effect $\Sigma k_i \dot{f}_i$	Differential effect $\Sigma k_i \dot{r}_i$	Industry ranking effect $\Sigma k_i \dot{s}_i$
1970–1	−0.591	0.746	−0.050	−1.240
1971–2	2.001	−0.163	2.778	−0.538
1972–3	−0.531	0.087	0.323	−0.923
1973–4	2.234	−0.716	1.827	1.078
1974–5	8.323	2.018	6.403	−0.351
1975–6	3.449	0.265	2.796	0.397
1976–7	0.081	−0.021	0.438	−0.349
1977–8	−2.552	−0.180	−2.006	−0.405
1978–9	−1.139	0.040	−0.009	−1.138
1979–80	1.019	0.192	0.234	0.519

	By occupation			
Year	Total change $\dot{r}$	Structure effect $\Sigma k_i \dot{f}_i$	Differential effect $\Sigma k_i \dot{r}_i$	Occupation ranking effect $\Sigma k_i \dot{s}_i$
1970–1	–	–	–	–
1971–2	–	–	–	–
1972–3	–	–	–	–
1973–4	4.845	0.285	3.876	0.669
1974–5	4.523	0.652	4.497	−0.516
1975–6	3.503	−0.044	1.877	1.671
1976–7	1.427	0.083	2.413	−1.039
1977–8	−0.307	0.004	0.820	−1.112
1978–9	−1.846	−0.029	−0.114	−1.708
1979–80	1.668	0.117	0.568	0.964

Notes: (i) See notes to Table 2.4.
(ii) Since a new classification of occupations was introduced in 1973, no comparisons can be made prior to this year.

the occupations in which women were heavily represented, than to actual decreases in relative pay within these occupations.

It is instructive to analyse in detail the data for two particular occupations: 'clerical and related', the occupation in which relative employment expanded most during the period (25.7 per cent increase), and 'processing, making, repairing and related metal and electrical', the occupation in which relative employment contracted most (26.5 per cent decrease). As we can see in Table 2.6, despite very different histories in employment, both occupations are similar in their relative wage behaviour. In both cases for most of the years, relative pay within the occupation increased. In fact, the losses in the last two years for the contracting occupations are small compared with gains achieved previously. Another feature of the data is that while compositional effects (the combined influence of the terms $k_i \hat{f}_i$ and $k_i \hat{s}_i$) tend to dominate in the contracting occupation, wage effects (the influence of $k_i \hat{r}_i$) are predominant in the expanding occupation. Finally, the table shows very clearly the reason for the declines in average relative pay during the years 1977—8 and 1978—9 reported above. These are mostly compositional effects due to the overall decline in average pay in the occupation in which women are most heavily represented ('clerical and related'); once these compositional effects are accounted for, however, relative pay within the occupation increased even in those years.

The last question we want to look into, using this decompositional technique, concerns the evolution of relative pay within different age groups. Changes in the age pattern of female participation could be a significant avenue through which increases in average relative pay could have been achieved. The proportion of married women who return to the labour force after child bearing is today much larger than it was 15 years ago, and these women tend to be more educated (and thus command higher wages) than previously. But if this was the only source of improvement it would reflect poorly on the effects of the equal pay legislation, since it would imply that economic opportunities for women were still very much unchanged. It is reasonable to think that this is not the case and that at least part of the increased participation of women has been due to improved pay for their work.

Table 2.7 is useful for isolating these different effects. It is clear from the first column that during the period 1974—80 there have been important changes in the age structure of the female working population. The proportions of young and old women have decreased, probably due to increased levels of education and earlier retirement, and the proportions of women in the age range 18 to 39 has increased. But the most substantial

Table 2.6. The year-to-year change in relative pay in the most expanding and most contracting occupations

Year	Clerical and related			
	Total change $\dot{r}$	Structure effect $k_i \dot{f}_i$	Differential effect $k_i \dot{r}_i$	Industry ranking effect $k_i \dot{s}_i$
1973–4	3.046	1.623	0.611	0.765
1974–5	4.847	1.719	−0.631	3.709
1975–6	2.140	0.533	1.758	−0.159
1976–7	1.243	1.813	−0.962	−0.415
1977–8	−0.350	0.976	−1.300	−0.006
1978–9	−1.074	0.287	−1.384	0.030
1979–80	1.971	0.137	0.915	0.902

Year	Processing, making, repairing, etc.			
	Total change $\dot{r}$	Structure effect $k_i \dot{f}_i$	Differential effect $k_i \dot{r}_i$	Occupation ranking effect $k_i \dot{s}_i$
1973–4	−0.233	0.112	−0.044	−0.294
1974–5	−0.471	0.176	0.033	−0.641
1975–6	−0.042	0.158	−0.015	−0.174
1976–7	−0.000	0.076	−0.014	−0.055
1977–8	0.113	0.022	0.002	0.088
1978–9	0.097	−0.032	0.012	0.119
1979–80	−0.244	−0.095	−0.009	−0.145

Notes: See notes to Table 2.5.

increase is that of the group aged 30–9 which is mostly made up of mothers returning to work. This is confirmed by the rates of increase of female employment proportions; the proportion of women in the 30–9 age group increased by 12 per cent during the period considered, while the other three age groups with positive rates of change (18–20, 21–4 and 25–9) increased by 5.6, 4.0 and 5.8 per cent respectively. This change in the age structure has resulted in an improved relative wage (in fact, the level of salaries in the 30–9 age group was the highest in 1980), but too small to explain the 10.8 per cent increase experienced between 1976

Table 2.7. Decomposition of the proportional change in the relative wage by age groups (1974—80)

Age group	Structure effect $k_i\dot{f_i}$ (1)	Differential effect $k_i\dot{r_i}$ (2)	Age ranking effect $k_i\dot{s_i}$ (3)
Under 18	−0.881	0.207	0.119
18−20	0.551	0.723	0.175
21−4	0.590	1.252	−0.411
25−9	0.735	1.633	−0.332
30−9	1.980	2.277	0.098
40−9	−1.676	2.538	0.220
50−9	−0.728	1.669	0.051

$\dot{r} = 10.803$ $\Sigma k_i \dot{f_i} = 0.571$ $\Sigma k_i \dot{r_i} = 10.299$ $\Sigma k_i \dot{s_i} = -0.081$

Notes: (i) See notes to Table 2.4.
(ii) The wage variable used is for gross wages inclusive of overtime effects because no information exists on wages net of overtime by age.

and 1980. As column (2) of Table 2.7 shows, the overall increase in relative pay is almost totally explained by increases in relative pay within age groups. Relative to men, women were earning more in 1980 than in 1974 in all age groups and the gains were substantial particularly towards the end of the age profile. This suggests that, at least partly, the increase in participation may have been caused by improved wages being offered by women's work, and therefore that supply effects must be taken into account when evaluating the possible impact of the equal pay legislation.

Another feature that illustrates the sort of changes operated during this period of time is the shape of the age profile of earnings. While in 1974 the maximum level of wages were obtained in the age group 25—9, in 1980 the maximum is reached in the age group 30—9, which makes the female profile more similar to that of men (their maximum is reached in the age group 40—9). This suggests a genuine improvement in the types of job opportunities that women are now offered as compared with 1974. Another possible cause would be the cohort effects of a much better-educated labour force, but the span of time is too short for these effects to have any significant impact.[10]

The evidence examined consistently points towards a substantial improvement in female relative wages; but so far we have only considered average levels. Have all women shared equally in this improvement? This is the question we answer in the next section.

2.3 Distributional effects

The *New Earnings Survey* provides data on the median, upper and lower deciles and upper and lower quartiles of the distribution of wages. Therefore it is possible to measure the change in female relative wages at several points in the distribution. This information is a useful complement because an improvement in terms of mean relative wages, which is essentially what we have found in the previous section, could be shared very differently by women at different points in the distribution. The presumption exists (see Chiplin *et al.* (1980) p. 106) that the equal pay legislation may simply have cut off the lower tail of the female distribution of wages, without changing either its shape or its overall position. This would certainly be consistent with a narrowing of the male–female gap if measured in terms of average values, but it would also imply that most of the gains had been achieved at the lower end of the distribution.

The evidence from the *New Earnings Survey* suggest that this is not what has happened. Panel A of Charts 2.5 and 2.6 presents the cumulative distributions of male and female wages for manual and non-manual workers at the beginning and the end of the decade. They are plotted against the logarithm of wages, so equal horizontal distances between the distributions indicate equal proportional differences between wages. The wage distributions of manual workers for 1970 suggest that the relative difference between female and male wages was fairly uniform across the whole distribution. The corresponding distributions for 1980 are much nearer to each other than they were in 1970, as we would expect from the improvement in wages documented above, and the gap appears to have narrowed more or less uniformly across the distribution. If anything, it is the bottom part of the distribution which shows the smallest improvement. But the differences are too small to give them much weight. Chart 2.5 can be summarised easily. The proportional gap between female and male manual wages is very similar for low and high wages, and the improvement in female relative wages has not greatly altered this uniformity.

As Chart 2.6 shows, non-manual workers present a similar picture, although there are some differences worth emphasising. The proportional

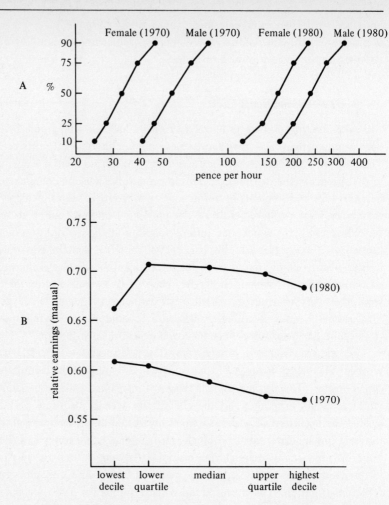

Chart 2.5 Changes in the distribution of wages for manual workers
A: Cumulative distribution of ln (W)
B: Ratio of female to male wages at different points of the distribution

gap is again fairly uniform at all levels of wages but larger than it was for manual workers, in both the initial and final years considered. While for manual workers the relative improvement in female relative wages was smallest for the lowest decile of the distribution, for non-manual workers this is the part of the distribution that does best.

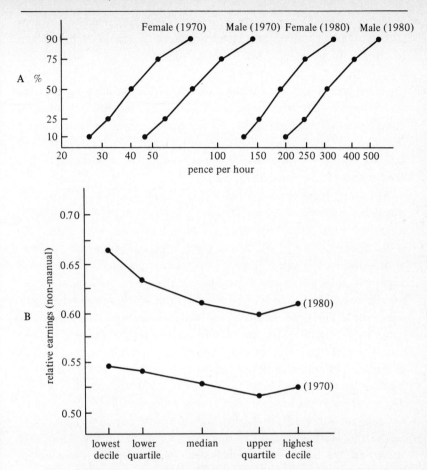

Chart 2.6 Changes in the distribution of wages for non-manual workers
A: Cumulative distribution of ln (*W*)
B: Ratio of female to male wages at different points of the distribution

2.4 Summary and conclusions

The evidence from the *New Earnings Survey* examined in this chapter suggests that there has been a substantial increase in the pay of women relative to that of men. This is true for both manual and non-manual workers and for full-time and part-time workers. When we look at the evolution of relative pay over the last decade we find that although these segments of the labour force have had fairly different employment histories, they all share the same behaviour as far as relative pay is concerned. In terms of female relative employment, the manual sector has contracted somewhat while the non-manual sector has clearly expanded, yet in both sectors the increase in female relative pay has been about the same. Further, not only the overall level but also the timing of this increase has been similar in both sectors. In general most of the gain was achieved in the period 1973—77, with moderate increases in the first and last years (1973—4 and 1976—7) and very large increases in the two middle years (1974—5 and 1975—6).

Was this improvement due just to compositional effects? Our conclusion is that it was not. We have examined in detail the extent to which the proportional increase in female relative wages was due to a redistribution of the female labour force towards high paying industries or occupations, the extent to which it was due to genuine improvement of wages within industries or occupations, and the extent to which it resulted from an overall improvement of those sectors in which women were highly represented. For both industries and occupations, and within those for both contracting and expanding sectors, we have always obtained the same conclusion: by far the major factor behind the improvement is an increase in relative pay within industries and within occupations. Even when we consider age groups we obtain the same result. Although there have been some changes in the age structure of the female working force, this does not account for much of the increase in relative pay. The main factor behind this increase is again an improvement in relative pay within each age group. We believe this improvement in pay may be a reason why married women are now returning to the labour force in greater numbers than in the past. It is interesting that despite this supply response, female relative pay has maintained the high levels reached in 1977.

The last piece of evidence that has been analysed is the distribution of wages. We were concerned that conclusions based only on comparisons of average wage levels might give a more optimistic picture than warranted, and wanted therefore to see how this improvement was shared by women at different points in the wage distribution. Our general conclusion is that the relative difference in wages between men and women has narrowed down fairly uniformly across the whole distribution.

3

Equal pay and the system of collective agreements

We have now looked in detail at the manner in which female relative pay has increased across industries and occupations. In this chapter we want to investigate the evolution of relative pay among those workers covered by collective agreements and, if possible, to compare this evolution with that of uncovered workers. This is an important issue because collective agreement is the most generalised form of pay determination in Britain,[11] and could well be the channel through which the rise in female relative pay has materialised.

In the first section of this chapter we look at some descriptive statistics of how relative pay has evolved in ten collective agreements (representing 46.4 per cent of the total number of covered workers, and 33.2 per cent of the total working population), and we attempt a comparison between covered and uncovered workers to see whether we can identify the channels through which the legislation has operated. If anti-discriminatory measures had been taken only through collective agreements, the extent and temporal pattern of relative wage increases among covered workers would be clearly different from that of uncovered workers.

In the second section we attempt a decomposition analysis, similar to that presented in the previous chapter, to see the extent to which relative pay has increased within agreements. The groups that we can identify on the basis of collective agreements data are more homogeneous than those based on industries or occupations, and this will allow us to investigate more closely what has happened in typically female sectors. If the degree of segregation is sufficiently high, one way of achieving equal pay could have been to reduce the pay of male workers in those sectors in which female employment is in the majority. This would result in an increase in the overall female relative pay, and yet it would be difficult to claim any success for the legislation. Finally, in the last section, we summarise the main findings of the chapter.

37

3.1 Relative pay among workers covered and uncovered by collective agreements

The system of pay determination in Britain is highly centralised. A relatively small number of collective agreements determine the rates of pay of a very large number of workers. In the early seventies, the 15 largest national agreements covered around $5\frac{1}{2}$ million workers, which represents around one-quarter of the total working population. A total of 3 million workers were covered by only four agreements. If in addition one considers wage orders, then the total number of covered workers is 14 million (63 per cent of the working population), of which 9 million are men (64 per cent of the male working population) and 5 million are women (61 per cent of the female working population).

It is therefore conceivable that the system of collective agreements has played an important role in implementing the equal pay legislation. Unions' and employers' representatives will have certainly found it very difficult to ignore the pressure imposed by the legislation on the equalisation of wage rates for men and women and this, as we shall see shortly, is what the data indicate. But it is still more relevant to see how employers have reacted to this equalisation of rates in terms of actual pay to women relative to men, and in terms of employment decisions. We leave the investigation of employment effects for the next chapter, and concentrate here on the impact of the legislation on wage rates and earnings.

In the first column of Table 3.1 we present female relative to male wage rates for full-time manual workers, and for the period 1950–80. The figures are obtained from data on minimum wage rates for covered workers, and are aggregated using the distribution of employment across collective agreements. Up to 1970 there was practically no variation in wage rates. For 20 years female minimum wage rates were on average about 18 per cent less than male rates. But this state of affairs began changing quite rapidly from 1971 onwards, to culminate in 1976 when full equality in rates was obtained.[12] The data show quite clearly that already in 1971, which corresponds to the first year of the adjustment period to the new legislation, there was a noticeable effect on relative rates of pay.

How did actual earnings react to this increase in rates? The answer is given in columns (2) and (3) of Table 3.1. Column (2) shows relative hourly earnings, and column (3) is an index of the ratio of column (2) over column (3). If, relative to men, female actual earnings had increased less

Table 3.1. Relative hourly earnings and relative hourly wage rates of full-time manual employees (1950–80)

Year	Relative hourly wage rates (1) (1976 = 100)	Relative hourly earnings (2)	Relative hourly earnings/ relative hourly wage rates (3) (1976 = 100)
1950	79.4	61.5	108.7
1951	80.7	61.7	107.3
1952	80.3	62.3	108.8
1953	81.3	61.6	106.3
1954	81.3	60.9	105.1
1955	80.8	60.5	105.0
1956	81.2	60.5	104.5
1957	81.4	60.4	104.1
1958	81.8	60.5	103.8
1959	81.9	60.7	104.0
1960	82.0	60.5	103.5
1961	82.2	60.2	102.7
1962	82.4	60.5	103.0
1963	82.9	60.2	101.9
1964	83.1	59.8	101.0
1965	83.5	59.5	100.0
1966	84.4	59.9	99.6
1967	84.4	59.7	99.2
1968	83.8	59.5	99.6
1969	83.3	59.5	100.2
1970	82.6	60.1	102.1
1971	84.9	60.6	100.1
1972	85.6	60.7	99.5
1973	87.4	62.5	100.3
1974	92.1	67.0	102.1
1975	95.1	68.0	100.3
1976	100.0	71.3	100.0
1977	100.0	71.8	100.1
1978	100.0	70.8	99.3
1979	100.0	70.7	99.2
1980	100.0	69.7	97.8

Notes: Hourly wage rates have been estimated as the weighted average of minimum rates laid down in collective agreements.
Source: *Department of Employment Gazette, British Historical Abstract, Annual Abstract of Statistics.*

than female wage rates, we would observe in the last column a substantial decline of the index over the last decade considered. But this is not the case. After 1970 there exists a mild downward trend, but it is both very weak and not substantially different from the falling tendency that the index already showed before 1970. Thus, we conclude that the increase in female rates was to a great extent translated into earnings.

The data just considered refer only to manual employees, but the evidence is sufficiently clear to indicate that the increase in wage rates had an impact on the real welfare of women. Furthermore, the data on earnings shown in column (2) refer to both covered and uncovered workers, which suggests that the effect was not just limited to employees covered by collective agreements. This cannot be verified precisely on the basis of these aggregated data, and it would be interesting to be able to compare actual earnings separately in the two sectors. The increase in relative pay shown in column (2) of Table 3.1 could have come from a much larger increase in relative pay among covered workers coupled with constant, or even falling, relative earnings among non-covered workers.

Table 3.2 shows that this is not the case. For manual workers it is true that between 1973 and 1978 relative earnings increased more among covered than among non-covered workers (17.9 per cent as compared to 15.6 per cent), but the difference is very small. The 15.6 per cent increase of female relative earnings in the non-covered sector indicates quite clearly that the legislation also had an important effect for these workers. Another corroborative piece of evidence is given by the relative position of women in these two sectors. Female relative earnings increased slightly more in the covered sector, but the ratio of female earnings in the covered sector over female earnings in the non-covered sector actually fell between 1973 and 1978 (by 1.1 per cent).[13]

The data for non-manual workers again confirm the hypothesis that the legislation was effective in both covered and non-covered sectors. Here, the increase in relative earnings in the non-covered sector was even higher than that in the covered sector (16.7 per cent as compared to 12.3 per cent). Also, as for manual workers, the position of women in the covered sector deteriorated when compared to that of women in the non-covered sector.

Putting the evidence of Tables 3.1 and 3.2 together we conclude that wage rates, as determined by collective agreements, started to move towards equalisation quite early in the decade, that these increases in

Table 3.2. Gross weekly earnings (£) of covered and non-covered employees
Excluding those whose pay was affected by absence

	1973			1978			Percentage change in relative pay
	Female	Male	Relative × 100	Female	Male	Relative × 100	
Manual							
Non-covered	17.4	34.4	50.6	43.9	75.0	58.5	15.6
Covered	20.7	38.9	53.2	51.7	82.4	62.7	17.9
All	19.7	38.1	51.7	49.4	80.7	61.2	18.4
Non-manual							
Non-covered	21.5	50.0	43.0	51.3	102.2	50.2	16.7
Covered	26.4	46.9	56.3	63.0	99.6	63.2	12.3
All	24.7	48.1	51.4	59.1	100.7	58.7	14.2
Manual and non-manual	23.1	41.9	55.1	56.4	89.1	63.3	14.9

Source: Gregory and Thomson (1981)

relative rates resulted in corresponding (and contemporaneous) increases
in relative earnings, and that the effect on earnings was not confined to
the covered sector but also spilled over to non-covered employees. It is
difficult, without more detailed data, to say anything on the precise timing
in which these events took place. If, as there are reasons to believe, the
collective agreement machinery was the main channel through which the
legislation was implemented, then we would have expected the increase
in relative earnings to show up earlier among covered than among non-
covered workers. But the data on earnings in Table 3.1 are too aggregate
to be helpful in this respect, and those of Table 3.2 give information only
for the year 1978, by which time most of the influence that collective
agreements may have had on non-covered workers would, in all probability,
have already been exerted.

3.2 Relative earnings within collective agreements

In the previous chapter we have seen that most of the increase in relative
pay has been due to genuine increases within sectors rather than to
compositional effects. It would be interesting to repeat the exercise, but
now using collective agreements rather than industries or occupations.
Some of these agreements cover a very homogeneous population of
workers, and this will allow us to check whether increases in relative pay
have been achieved not so much by increasing female wages but by
lowering male pay in those sectors in which women are the majority.

We have been able to collect data on earnings and employment for the
period 1972 to 1980 for ten collective agreements, which cover a fairly
large segment of the covered population. In some of them, like clerical
grades in the Civil Service, non-manual workers covered by the wage
boards, and ancillary staff in the National Health Service, the proportion
of female workers is very high. If the increase in relative pay has been
achieved by lowering men's pay, we should observe that for these
agreements the third term in the decomposition formula (2.2) (see Chapter
2) is both negative and large relative to the other terms.

In Table 3.3 we present the results of decomposing the percentage
increase in relative pay between 1972 and 1980 into that part of the
increase due to movements in the distribution of female employment
between agreements ($\Sigma k_i \dot{f_i}$), that part due to relative wage increases within
agreements ($\Sigma k_i \dot{r_i}$), and that part due to changes in the relative position of

the agreement as measured by changes in men's wages ($\Sigma k_i \dot{s}_i$). The first three columns present the decomposition including all the ten agreements available, and the next three columns the same decomposition but excluding teachers in primary and secondary schools. The first decomposition shows that although there is a negative effect coming from a decline in men's wages (column 3), this is smaller than that coming from the increase in relative pay within agreements (column 2). Furthermore, it is clear that most of this negative effect comes from a deterioration of the wages of male teachers, who belong to an agreement in which equal pay was already in force since 1961. Thus, this negative effect cannot be due to the manner in which equal pay was implemented, but rather to other causes concerning changes in the relative position of teaching. In fact, during this decade there was a substantial expansion of teaching, which only on account of changes in the distribution across its occupational salary structure could have resulted in some fall in the relative position of male teachers. This expansion is also seen in the large compositional effect that this agreement has (column 1). Since, on average, women are paid more in teaching than elsewhere, the expansion of this occupation resulted in a very large increase in the overall female relative pay. It may therefore be more adequate to repeat the exercise excluding teaching, which as mentioned above had, after all, already implemented equal pay.

Columns (4) to (6) of Table 3.3 show the results of this new exercise. Overall, the data do not support the hypothesis that the increase in relative pay was achieved by lowering men's rather than raising women's pay. For instance, non-manual workers covered by wage boards, with 67 per cent of female employment, show a substantial increase in relative pay within the agreement, and yet men's relative position in this sector improved slightly. The same is true of ancillary workers in the National Health Service, which has a 61 per cent proportion of female employment. Relative pay also improved there, and the data do not suggest that this was achieved by decreases in men's pay.

In Table 3.4 we decompose the year to year increase in relative pay for all the ten collective agreements (columns 1 to 4), and for the nine agreements after excluding teaching (columns 5 to 8). The picture is very similar to that discussed in Table 2.6 for industries and occupations. Particularly after excluding the large compositional effects coming from teaching, we find that the within agreement effects are in general the dominant ones, and that the largest improvements were those obtained in the three-year period 1973–1976.

Table 3.3. Decomposition of the proportional change in relative (f/m) wages by selected collective agreements (1972–80)

Agreement	All agreements available		
	Structure effect $k_i \dot{f}_i$ (1)	Differential effect $k_i \dot{r}_i$ (2)	Agreement ranking effect $k_i \dot{s}_i$ (3)
1. Engineering (M)	−4.308	1.904	−0.715
2. Engineering (N)	−3.259	1.490	0.087
3. Retail co-op (M−N)	−0.353	−0.007	0.020
4. Wages board (M)	−5.254	2.921	−1.204
5. Wages board (N)	2.258	2.725	−0.525
6. Local authorities (M)	0.621	0.292	0.257
7. Civil servants–clerical	4.985	0.532	−0.629
8. Government industrial establishments (M)	0.377	0.192	−0.052
9. Ancillary, NHS (M−N)	0.321	0.705	−0.099
10. Teachers	17.037	2.047	−4.415
	$\Sigma k_i \dot{f}_i = 12.425$	$\Sigma k_i \dot{r}_i = 12.801$	$\Sigma k_i \dot{s}_i = -7.275$

$\dot{r}$ 14.305

Agreement	Excluding teachers		
	Structure effect $k_i f_i$ (4)	Differential effect $k_i r_i$ (5)	Agreement ranking effect $k_i s_i$ (6)
1. Engineering (M)	−6.163	3.106	−0.428
2. Engineering (N)	−4.977	2.429	0.589
3. Retail co-op (M−N)	−0.316	−0.012	0.199
4. Wages board (M)	−6.690	4.763	−0.662
5. Wages board (N)	6.269	4.443	0.259
6. Local authorities (M)	1.872	0.476	0.835
7. Civil servants−clerical	10.282	0.868	−0.365
8. Government industrial establishments (M)	0.843	0.313	−0.002
9. Ancillary, NHS (M−N)	1.321	1.150	0.217
	$\Sigma k_i f_i = 2.441$	$\Sigma k_i r_i = 17.536$	$\Sigma k_i s_i = 0.642$

$\bar{r}$ 19.272

Notes: (i) See notes to Tables 2.3 and 2.4; and Annex to Chapter 3.
(ii) M, manual; N, non-manual; M−N, both.
Source: New Earnings Survey, 1972, 1980.

Table 3.4. Decomposition of the year-to-year proportional changes in the wage differential by collective agreements, (1972–80)

Year	All agreements available			
	Total change $\dot{r}$ (1)	Structure effect $\Sigma k_i \dot{f_i}$ (2)	Differential effect $\Sigma k_i \dot{r_i}$ (3)	Agreement ranking effect $\Sigma k_i \dot{s_i}$ (4)
1972–3	−0.18	1.79	0.42	−2.15
1973–4	3.42	−2.31	3.72	1.78
1974–5	9.19	8.95	3.10	−2.38
1975–6	6.71	1.93	3.94	0.92
1976–7	−0.91	0.24	1.00	−1.86
1977–8	−0.70	0.23	−0.43	−0.49
1978–9	−3.94	0.95	−0.01	−4.69
1979–80	0.53	0.07	0.34	0.06

Year	Excluding teachers			
	Total change $\dot{r}$ (5)	Structure effect $\Sigma k_i \dot{f_i}$ (6)	Differential effect $\Sigma k_i \dot{r_i}$ (7)	Agreement ranking effect $\Sigma k_i \dot{s_i}$ (8)
1972–3	0.12	1.04	0.76	−1.39
1973–4	6.52	0.48	4.83	0.95
1974–5	5.79	2.17	4.64	−0.15
1975–6	3.91	0.65	3.92	1.16
1976–7	2.18	0.67	0.92	1.09
1977–8	−0.19	0.11	−0.87	0.59
1978–9	−3.96	−1.03	−0.72	−2.29
1979–80	2.54	0.02	0.76	1.64

Notes: See notes to Table 2.4.

3.3 Summary and conclusions

From this review of the data on collective agreements we conclude that the machinery of pay determination in Britain may have played an important role in the implementation of equal pay. Although we have not been able to establish precisely the timing in which increases in relative pay took place in the covered and non-covered sectors, we have shown that relative wage rates as determined by collective agreements started increasing in a noticeable manner as early as 1971, and were almost equal by the end of the adjustment period to the new legislation. Relative earnings in the whole economy followed a similar evolution, which makes us think that, at least in the covered sector, female relative pay also started increasing well before the date at which the Equal Pay Act and the Sex Discrimination Act became law (end of 1975).

We would have expected that steps towards equalisation of pay in the non-covered sector would be taken later than in the covered sector, as there was no legal compulsion to act otherwise before 1976, nor was there any commitment through collective negotiation. The aggregated data on relative earnings in Table 3.1, however, do not seem to indicate any noticeable lag between the evolution of relative earnings. Also, as shown by Table 3.2, it is clear that whatever difference in the evolution of relative pay may have existed between covered and non-covered sectors, that divergency had completely disappeared by 1978. By this time relative earnings in the non-covered sector had increased more than in the covered sector for non-manual workers, and by only about 2 per cent less for manual workers. Also in both cases, female pay in the non-covered sector had improved relative to female pay in the covered sector.

We can see then that the impact of the legislation has been widespread. It may have used the machinery of collective agreements as its main channel of implementation, but it seems clear that it also had a similar, and probably quite contemporaneous effect on workers not covered by these agreements.

Finally, we have attempted to see if within agreements, particularly within agreements in which female employment is substantial, equal pay had been obtained by lowering men's earnings rather than by increasing women's pay. If the degree of segregation is sufficiently large, this could have been one way of achieving equal pay for equal work; an achievement probably quite contrary to the intentions of the legislator. We have satisfied ourselves that this was not the case. The only substantial fall in the relative position of men's earnings is found for teachers, who were already enjoying equal pay. In all other agreements, very large increases in female relative pay were accompanied by either very small falls or by actual improvements in men's relative position.

In this and the previous chapter we have tried to assess the impact of the equal pay legislation by looking at different aspects of the evolution of relative pay, but we have not considered any factors other than this legislation that may have also had an influence on the relative position of female workers. Before we are able to substantiate the conclusion that equal pay has had a significant positive effect, we need to consider the labour market as a whole, taking into account not only relative employment but also other forces that, through their effect on demand and supply, may have had an impact on relative pay. We turn to this task in the next chapter.

4

The effect of anti-discriminatory legislation on relative pay and employment

The substantial increase in female relative pay has already been documented in Chart 1.1. Between 1970 and 1980 female relative hourly earnings rose by 14.8 per cent and, as Chapter 2 shows, the increase affected quite similarly all occupations and industries. There was also a remarkable similarity in the timing of this increase. In practically all sectors, most of the gains in female pay were achieved in the period 1974–6. It is certainly tempting to attribute this increase to the anti-discriminatory legislation enacted in Britain around that time. The Equal Pay Act, requiring equal pay for equivalent work by men and women, was passed in 1970 but its application was delayed until the end of 1975 to allow employers time to adjust to the new set of conditions on pay. The end of 1975 was also the time at which the Sex Discrimination Act, requiring equal employment opportunities for men and women, became law. Thus there exists a very clear coincidence between the increase in relative pay and the application of this legislation.

A coincidence, however, is not sufficient to establish that the anti-discriminatory legislation was the main contributory factor behind the increase in female relative pay. There are other factors, which also changed during this period, and which could be the cause of this increase quite independently of legislation. One such factor, which has been put forward by some authors (Chiplin *et al.*, 1980) as a possible cause of the increase in female relative pay, is the effect of the various incomes policies applied in Britain during the seventies. Some of them had flat rate provisions which could have benefited women to a larger extent than men. Another factor which could possibly explain the rise in female relative pay would be an autonomous decrease in the supply of female labour. Here, however, the evidence does not seem too corroborative. Overall, as Chart 1.2 suggests, there has been an impressive increase in the number of women in the labour force during the seventies. Between 1970 and 1980, female relative employment increased by 18.3 per cent, and relative man-hours by 17.6 per cent.

In this chapter we put all these factors together. We shall attempt an evaluation of the possible effects of anti-discriminatory legislation by considering the labour market as a whole, taking into account not only relative employment but also other factors that, through their influence on demand and supply, may have affected relative pay. The prima-facie evidence in favour of the effectiveness of this legislation is very strong, and we wish to see if this evidence is maintained after considering all these additional factors and their interaction within the context of the labour market. In the first section we discuss two possible theoretical approaches for the analysis of this question, and in the second section we discuss the empirical specifications used. The third section presents the empirical results obtained, and the fourth summarises the argument and conclusions.

4.1 Theoretical considerations

We begin the analysis by positing a demand relationship of the form

$$\frac{W_f}{W_m} = f\left(\frac{E_f}{E_m}\right) \tag{4.1}$$

where W_f/W_m is female relative wages and E_f/E_m is relative employment. The economic rationale behind the negative relationship (4.1) is taken from Becker's work on discrimination (Becker, 1971). If men and women had equal productivity and if there was no discrimination by employers, a competitive market would set $W_f = W_m$ irrespective of relative quantities supplied to the market. (The overall level of wages would of course depend on the *total* supply of men and women). If, on the other hand, employers discriminate against women, then $W_f \neq W_m$, since they will equate women's marginal product not to their wage but to their wage plus a mark-up that captures their degree of discrimination against this type of labour. If this mark-up is positive, $W_f < W_m$. But this is not yet sufficient to generate the relationship (4.1). If the discriminatory attitudes of all employers were the same, a differential between men's and women's wages would arise, but this differential would be independent of relative quantities. If, on the other hand, attitudes towards discrimination differ across employers, a negative relationship would be observed. For a given number of women in the labour market, there will be a distribution of female employment, with the majority of women employed in sectors in which discrimination is small and a minority in sectors in which discrimination is large. But, as more women enter the labour market, they will have to deal more and more frequently with highly discriminatory employers, and this will lower the relative wage. Thus the negative relationship between relative wages and relative employment posited by (4.1). The position of this relationship will depend on the average market discrimination, and its slope on the variance of discrimination between employers. If the variance is small the demand curve will tend to be flat, with equality in discriminating preferences generating a horizontal demand curve. Then, the relative wage differential is completely determined by demand forces. If the variance is large, the demand curve will tend to be vertical, with small increases in female labour forcing women to seek employment with highly discriminatory employers and thus lowering substantially the relative wage. Then, supply forces will matter in the determination of the relative wage differential.[14]

The existence of tastes for discrimination is not the only reason that can generate relationship (4.1). We only need to postulate that men and women are not perfect substitutes in demand, for a negative relationship between relative wages and relative employment to arise. This would require that employers took men and women of equal measurable characteristics, such as education, training and labour market experience, as factors which are different as far as production is concerned. The best-known explanation for this behaviour advanced in the literature concerns the effect that information costs may have in determining actual levels of productivity. If information is costly and measurable attributes such as education are poor indicators of skill, employers may take other characteristics such as race or sex as proxies for expected productivity, and thus treat men and women (or blacks and whites) with the same level of education as different factors in production (Phelps, 1972; Aigner and Cain, 1977).

Previous studies on the effect of anti-discriminatory legislation have tended to follow Becker's model of discrimination, and have concentrated mostly on the impact of racial anti-discriminatory measures in the United States (Landes, 1968; Ashenfelter, 1970; Freeman, 1973; Butler and Heckman, 1977). In the context of this model the effect of anti-discriminatory legislation is to make it more costly for employers to indulge in discriminatory practices. After the legislation is passed, therefore, we should observe fewer discriminating employers than previously, and possibly a smaller degree of discrimination among those who still violate the law. The end result would be an increase in relative female wages, at any given level of relative female employment, and therefore an increase in the overall demand for female relative to male labour.[15]

Financial penalties for breaking anti-discriminatory legislation are not as important in the United Kingdom as they are in the United States, and it is doubtful that they have played any important role in changing employers behaviour in this country. As we have seen in Chapter 3, the machinery of collective agreements may have been much more effective in actually raising female relative pay than fear of prosecution. The Equal Pay Act explicitly provided for the removal of discrimination (by abolishing differentiated female rates) in the pay structures determined by collective agreements and statutory wage orders, and the wide degree of coverage must have meant a rise in the relative price of female labour for many employers. But if, for any reason, employers did not respond to this increase by reducing female employment (that is, if they were prepared to hire the same number of women at higher relative wages), then the result of the legislation would have been again an increase in the relative demand for female labour. It is difficult to be precise about the reasons that could explain this behaviour, but the combination of sizeable turnover costs, likely deterioration of industrial relations and possible union reprisals were probably significant enough to prevent employers from undertaking large adjustments in the composition of their labour force.

Therefore under both explanations we could represent the effect of the anti-discriminatory legislation by an upward shift of the relative demand for female labour. This, of course, is not the only view that could be taken; the legislation could have also operated by just altering relative factor prices under unchanged demand conditions. The legislation would act as a minimum wage provision and, rather than inducing a movement of the whole demand curve for relative female employment, it would induce a movement along this demand curve. However, for this to be the case it would be necessary that the only enforced aspect of the legislation was its equal pay provision (Equal Pay Act). Then we would expect firms to reduce the amount of female labour by laying off women, very much the same as we expect a reduction in the employment of youth labour as a result of minimum wage legislation. But, the legislation has also an equal employment opportunities provision (Sex Discrimination Act) which makes this result uncertain. As a result of this provision it is illegal to treat women less favourably than men as far as employment, training and promotion decisions are concerned, and this would prevent employers from segregating their labour forces.[16] In the context of this model and at this level of generality, it is difficult to predict precisely the effect of this additional constraint on the relative demand curve, but we would expect it to have similar consequences as those considered in the context of Becker's model (a rightward displacement of the whole relationship), or at least to result in an increase of the relative level of female labour employed.

With regard to the econometric analysis that we develop in Section 4.3, the main implication of these two views on the effect of anti-discriminatory legislation concerns the treatment of relative wages. According to the first approach, relative wages should be treated as an endogenous variable, whose level will be determined by the joint effect of demand and supply. The main channel of operation of the legislation is through demand, and the resulting level of relative wages (as well as that of employment) will depend both on the expected displacement of the relative demand curve and on the shape and possible autonomous changes that may have occurred to supply. This is essentially an equilibrium framework in which both relative wages and relative employment are assumed sufficiently flexible to adjust over the period considered, and in which the main effect of the legislation is to change employers' behaviour.

The second approach, on the other hand, would treat relative wages as an exogenous variable. For equal productive characteristics female wages should equal male wages; thus the law effectively fixes the level of the relative wage at unity. The effect of the equal pay aspect of the legislation then takes the form of a movement along the relative demand curve, implying a decrease in the relative amount of female labour. But this does not necessarily mean that demand is unaffected by the legislation; to the extent that the equal employment opportunities provision has an influence, this approach would represent this additional aspect of the law by a displacement of the demand curve which, by assumption, could have an effect on the level of relative employment.

Since there is no obvious a priori reason to favour one approach over the other, in the empirical analysis below we estimate both of them and attempt to evaluate their appropriateness on statistical grounds. Both empirical models aim at estimating only the demand relationship (4.1),[17] but in the first we represent the anti-discriminatory legislation by means of a dummy variable D affecting the position of the relationship and treat both relative employment and relative wages as endogenous variables. This means that in the context of this model we must also specify the variables that, in addition to relative wages, determine relative supply (we discuss below some of the facts that may influence relative supply). If we represent the demand function by $d(.)$ and the supply function by $s(.)$, the system of equations underlying this first model is

$$\frac{W_f}{W_m} = d\left(\frac{E_f}{E_m}, D\right) \tag{4.2}$$

$$\frac{E_f}{E_m} = s\left(\frac{W_f}{W_m}\right) \tag{4.3}$$

with $d_1 < 0, d_2 > 0$ and $s_1 > 0$ (we represent the partial derivative of each of these functions with respect to the ith variable by d_i and s_i).

The second empirical model estimates again the relative demand relationship (4.1) but treats the relative wage as an exogenous variable. Then the underlying model is fully described by the demand equation only, since the exogenous increases in relative wages will be presumed to trace the demand relationship.[18] Expressing now the demand curve with the (single) endogenous variable on the left hand side, the model is

$$\frac{E_f}{E_m} = g\left(\frac{W_f}{W_m}, D\right) \tag{4.4}$$

with $g_1 < 0$ and $g_2 > 0$. In (4.4) the effect of D captures the influence on relative employment exerted by the equal employment opportunities provision of the legislation.

4.2 Empirical specification

The specifications of the demand and supply equations given so far are very general. We consider now other variables that may occur in such equations, the specific way in which all these variables are defined and the form that the aggregate demand relationship would take.

The relative wage variable is defined as relative hourly earnings of manual and non-manual employees. The relative employment variable is defined as total woman-hours divided by total man-hours for manual and non-manual employees, and includes female part-time employment. These variables are plotted in Charts 1.1 and 1.2, and their exact calculation and sources of these and other variables are given in the Annex to this chapter.

The demand function that we wish to estimate is an aggregate relationship and compositional changes could affect the relative level of female employment quite independently of any price influence. For instance, during the period in question due to autonomous changes (e.g. changes in tastes, external demand, technical innovations) some sectors could have expanded more than others. If the sectors that have expanded more are intensive in the employment of female labour, then we would observe an increase in the relative amount of female labour employed, due only to this change in the structure of the economy. Ideally we would like to isolate the effect that changes in relative wages have on relative employment for a given industrial structure, and we can do this by holding constant the distribution of male employment over the period. We call this index of industrial structure I and we define it as

$$ I_t = \sum_{i=1}^{n} A_i \frac{M_{it}}{M_t} \tag{4.5} $$

where M_{it} is the employment of male workers in sector i in year t, M_t is total employment in year t, n is the number of sectors considered and the values of A are time invariant weights. These weights are obtained as the average of the female—male wage bill ratio during the period 1970—80, although an alternative definition using only 1980 data gave practically identical results.[19]

Demand for female relative to male labour is likely to increase during upturns in economic activity. Due to its relatively short attachment to the labour force, female labour is likely to have less specific training than male labour and thus to experience more employment fluctuations over the cycle. This view, first explicitly stated by Becker (1964), implies that a variable measuring the cycle should also be included as an argument of the demand function. We represent this variable by the relative deviation of gross domestic product from a linear trend, and we call it (Q/Q^*), where Q is actual GDP and Q^* is trend GDP.[20]

The theoretical arguments, considered above, to generate the demand relationship are valid if men and women have equal productivity (otherwise there would not be much point in talking of discrimination). Thus, if there exist differences in productivity by sex, these should be taken into account in specifying the demand equation. One way of standard-ising for this would be to enter relative levels of education as a proxy of relative levels of productivity; but the problem here is that it is dif-ficult to obtain a long enough series of annual data. Nevertheless, temporal changes in this variable have been smooth and its influence (plus that of other unidentified factors) is likely to be well captured by a simple time trend, which we denote by T.[21]

As discussed above, British anti-discriminatory legislation consists of two Acts (Equal Pay and Sex Discrimination) both of which became law on the last day of 1975. The Equal Pay Act, however, had been passed five years earlier, and the interim period was conceded to allow employers to make the necessary changes in pay practices in a uniform and gradual manner. Thus, rather than only specifying the anti-discriminatory legislation dummy as one variable taking the value 0 up to 1975 and 1 afterwards, we allowed also several other specifications which could capture a more gradual effect. After some experimentation, the specification that best fitted the data was a set of four dummy variables which measure the *cumulative* effect of the legislation during the years 1971, 1972, 1974, and 1975. The dummy corresponding to the year 1971, $D71$, takes the value 0 up to 1970 and the value 1 afterwards. $D72$ takes the value 0 up to 1971 and the value 1 afterwards, and so on.

Another variable that must be included in the demand function is a dummy for incomes policies. To the extent that incomes policies have been equalising (through their flat rate provisions, in those cases in which such provisions have been present), they may have contributed to the increase of female relative wages. If Chiplin *et al.* (1980) are correct, this dummy should be more important in explaining shifts in the demand curve than the dummy representing anti-discriminatory legislation. We call this variable *IP*.

We initially tried two alternative incomes policy dummies. The first took the value 1 during all the periods in which there has been a compulsory incomes policy in effect, whatever its type, and the value 0 otherwise. This gives a value 1 for the years 1967 to 1969 (both inclusive), the year 1973 and the years 1976 to 1978 (both inclusive). But this formulation brings together incomes policies which were of a proportional type, and therefore ought not to have any equalising effect, and incomes policies with flat rate provisions which had potentially equalising effects. Since the latter are the ones that may have had an effect on female relative earnings, the specification finally used in the empirical analysis takes the value 1 only during the year 1973 and the years 1976 to 1978 (both inclusive). As we would expect the latter specification performs better than the first one in all cases.

Taking all these variables into account, the demand equation that will be estimated is

$$\ln\left(\frac{W_f}{W_m}\right) = \alpha_0 + \alpha_1 \ln\left(\frac{FH}{MH}\right) + \alpha_2 \ln(I) + \alpha_3 \ln\left(\frac{Q}{Q^*}\right) +$$

$$\alpha_4 T + \alpha_5 D + \alpha_6 IP + u \tag{4.6}$$

where α is the value of the parameters to be estimated, $\ln(.)$ is the logarithmic function, FH/MH is woman-hours relative to man-hours and u is a random error.

To estimate (4.6) when both relative employment and relative wages are considered endogenous, we must also take into account those factors that determine these two endogenous variables via the supply function, and use them as additional instruments in the estimation of the demand relationship.

The economic variables most frequently considered in cross-sectional studies of female participation are own female wages and other income. In the case of married women, most of 'other income' is made up of husband's earnings, which in our case is already captured by the presence of W_m and need not be explicitly considered. But we use as an instrument, aggregate disposable non-labour real income Y, to detect any additional effect coming from dividend income or interest on savings. The second variable that we consider is a fertility index FI; the number and age of children are the most important determinants of female participation in cross-sectional studies, and should also be important in a time-series context.[22] Here we define this index as the number of live births in the last five years per thousand women. Finally, we use as an instrument the rate of male unemployment U, which appears to have a significant influence in time-series studies of female participation, through what are known as the 'added and discouraged worker effects' (Mincer, 1966).

4.3 Results

In Table 4.1 we show the results of estimating the demand function using two-stage least squares (2SLS) under the assumption that the correct model underlying the relationship between employment and pay is that given by equations (4.2) and (4.3). In the first column, the dummy variables are not included and the results are quite unsatisfactory. The relationship between relative employment and relative pay is positive and significant, which is contrary to what we would expect on theoretical grounds. Additionally, we see that the Durbin–Watson statistic is very low, thus suggesting that the equation may be mis-specified. Things do not improve much when we add the incomes policy dummy *IP* in column (2); if anything, the significance of the positive relationship between earnings and employment is reinforced. But when we include the set of anti-discriminatory legislation dummies in column (3) the results change substantially. First, the relationship between relative pay and relative employment turns negative as we would expect and also is statistically significant. Second, the Durbin–Watson statistic takes a much more satisfactory value and the fit of the regression improves substantially (the standard error of the regression goes down from 0.0194 to 0.0079, with a mean value of the dependent variable equal to −0.4991). Finally, the added legislation dummies all take the expected values and are statistically significant.

Taking column (3) as our preferred specification we see that all variables, except perhaps the deviations of output from trend (Q/Q^*), take the expected sign. Relative demand, $\ln(FH/MH)$, is negatively related to relative pay and significant at the 5 per cent level. The results suggest a fairly elastic relative demand curve, with a wage elasticity equal to −3.81, which in turn implies the existence of a relatively small degree of variation in discrimination tastes and/or a high degree of substitution between male and female labour. The coefficient of the industrial index takes a positive sign and is large and significant, suggesting that the change in the industrial structure has had an important effect on the rise of female over male employment. The considerable expansion of service relative to manufacturing sectors that has taken place over the period is consistent with this result. We would have expected Q/Q^* to have a positive coefficient, reflecting a higher relative demand for female labour in the upturn of the cycle, but the estimate obtained is negative, although

Table 4.1. 2SLS estimates of the demand relationship for the whole economy (1950–80)
Dependent variable ln (relative hourly earnings)
Mean dependent variable $= -0.4991$

Explanatory variables	Equation		
	(1)	(2)	(3)
Constant	0.8774	0.4266	0.1065
	(1.70)	(0.92)	(0.38)
$\ln(FH/MH)$	0.4366	0.4143	−0.2622
	(4.04)	(4.50)	(2.21)
$\ln(I)$	0.6785	0.3873	0.4493
	(1.77)	(1.13)	(2.31)
$\ln(Q/Q^*)$	−0.6613	−0.7082	−0.0965
	(5.11)	(6.37)	(1.08)
T	−0.0040	−0.0025	−0.0045
	(1.77)	(1.24)	(3.41)
$D71$			0.0224
			(2.08)
$D72$			0.0125
			(1.22)
$D74$			0.0594
			(4.14)
$D75$			0.0773
			(5.38)
IP		0.0374	0.0165
		(3.31)	(2.65)
DW	0.7555	1.2246	2.4369
Standard error of the regression	0.0194	0.0165	0.0079

Notes: (i) The additional instruments used were a fertility index, male unemployment and non-labour income.
(ii) Figures in brackets are absolute *t*-statistics.

insignificant. This could suggest the absence of cyclical effects on relative wages, but the result could also be due to the fact that labour heterogeneity has not been fully taken into account. As the level of economic activity increases, more women with below average pay may enter the labour force, and this would push down female relative earnings.

The legislation dummies show a positive and significant effect, even after the time trend, which has a small negative coefficient, and all other variables are taken into account. The results on these dummies suggest that the legislation began to have an influence quite early in the transitional period and that most of the effect took place precisely during this period, particularly during its last year. We tried a set of dummies covering the whole decade, but the only significant ones tended to be those included in the equation. It is interesting to compare these results with those obtained in Chapter 2 on the basis of *New Earnings Survey* data. There, without taking into account the joint influence of other variables, we estimate that the most substantial gains in female relative earnings were achieved in the years 1975 and 1976, with marginal improvements in 1974 and 1977. Here, on the other hand, we conclude that most of the increases in 1976 and 1977 were due to the effect of income policies, and that the anti-discriminatory legislation had its largest influence in the years 1974 and 1975.

The overall effect of legislation, as measured in column (3) of Table 4.1, has been to increase relative female earnings by 18.8 per cent, if the non-significant effect of 1972 is taken into account, or by 17.3 per cent if that effect is ignored.[23] The effect of incomes policy, on the other hand, is measured to be only 1.7 per cent. Chiplin *et al.* (1980) are therefore only partially correct. It is true that incomes policies explain part of the increase experienced by female relative earnings during the seventies, but this effect is only marginal when we compare it with that exerted by anti-discriminatory legislation.

The 18.8 per cent increase in relative female earnings as a result of anti-discriminatory legislation is a *ceteris paribus* effect. That is, it tells us by how much female relative earnings would have risen if everything else had remained constant. In terms of the demand relationship, it measures the vertical displacement of this function. However, other things have not remained constant and, in particular, there has been a substantial increase in the level of relative employment, which has meant a final increase in relative earnings somewhat below the 18.8 per cent level mentioned above. To see this in terms of the model used here, we show in Chart 4.1 the configuration of relative wages and employment before and after the legislation. Using column (3) in Table 4.1 to estimate the value of relative wages for the year 1970, we obtain $\ln(W_f/W_m) = -0.496$ (or $W_f/W_m = 0.609$), which together with the value of relative employment for this year, $\ln(F/M) = -0.810$ (or $F/M = 0.445$), determines point A. This point

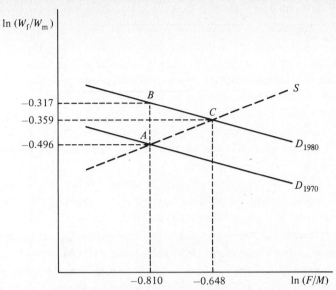

Chart 4.1 Relative wages and employment before and after the anti-discriminatory legislation (model with endogenous relative pay)

belongs to the demand relationship before the legislation (D_{1970}). We measure the position of the demand curve after legislation by re-evaluating relative wages, at the same level of relative employment but at the value for the year 1980 of the remaining variables. This yields the value $\ln(W_f/W_m) = -0.317$ (or $W_f/W_m = 0.729$), and gives the vertical shift of the demand curve from point A to point B. Between A and B, female relative wages increase by 19.7 per cent, of which 18.8 per cent is due to the anti-discriminatory legislation and 0.9 per cent to other factors. But point B is not the final position; the increase in relative wages, plus other factors operating through the supply side of the market, raise relative employment from $\ln(F/M) = -0.810$ to $\ln(F/M) = -0.648$ (or in terms of the F/M ratio from 0.445 to 0.523, the means for the years 1970 and 1980 respectively), and this depresses relative wages from $\ln(W_f/W_m) = -0.317$ to $\ln(W_f/W_m) = -0.359$ (or in terms of W_f/W_m, from 0.729 to 0.698). Point C in Chart 4.1 represents this final position, which we link to the initial position by a broken supply curve (not identified in our econometric analysis).[24] The actual increase in relative wages between 1970 and 1980 was 14.8 per cent, while the predicted increase is 14.6 per cent.

It could be argued that we have been able to isolate a positive effect of the legislation on the relative demand for female labour due to the fact that our analysis has included both the private and the public sector. Public employers are not necessarily cost minimisers and could have been the ones responsible for most of the huge rise in female employment, despite the substantial increase in female wages. This would imply that the anti-discriminatory legislation had operated only through a rather narrow channel, with little effect among private employers. It is therefore important to repeat the exercise above, excluding this time the public sector.

Ideally we would have liked to define for the private sector all the variables used in the previous estimation, but due to data difficulties it is not possible to obtain these variables for the whole of the period considered. So we repeat the exercise in Table 4.1, redefining only the relative employment and industrial structure variables, which are obtained as above but excluding the following industries: mining, transport, utilities (gas, electricity and water), professional and scientific services and public administration. This is not totally satisfactory because there are some private employers among the excluded industries and some public employers among those that remain. Nevertheless the new variables are likely to pick up reasonably well the evolution of female relative employment in the private sector during the period considered. Relative wages, on the other hand, could not be obtained for the private sector alone, and we must conform with the previously defined variable. Thus, the results of this exercise cannot be taken as conclusive, but they are useful in that they can indicate whether there exists any important difference in the effects of the legislation between private and public sectors.

The estimates of this exercise, presented in Table 4.2, suggest quite clearly that, on the basis of these data, it is not possible to detect any dramatic divergency in the effect of the legislation between the private and public sectors. Despite the fact the relative employment in the private sector behaves quite differently from that in the public sector, the effect of the legislation dummies is very similar in its timing and somewhat larger in magnitude. The *ceteris paribus* effect of the legislation is now 19.6 per cent, as compared to 18.8 per cent when the public sector was also included. We also find very similar effects for relative wages and for incomes policy. The only difference concerns the effect of changes in the industrial structure, which are much weaker when the private sector is

Table 4.2. 2SLS estimates of the demand relationship for the private sector (1950–80)
Dependent variable ln (relative hourly earnings)
Mean dependent variable $= -0.4991$

Explanatory variables	Equation		
	(1)	(2)	(3)
Constant	0.0936	−0.0334	−0.3552
	(0.31)	(0.14)	(3.17)
ln(FH/MH)	0.5676	0.4676	−0.2454
	(5.06)	(5.39)	(2.27)
ln(I^*)	0.4728	0.3194	0.1521
	(1.36)	(1.30)	(1.32)
ln(Q/Q^*)	−0.5116	−0.6138	−0.0480
	(3.01)	(4.56)	(.58)
T	0.0047	0.0036	−0.0035
	(8.38)	(7.47)	(3.51)
D71			0.0240
			(2.43)
D72			0.0171
			(1.58)
D74			0.0508
			(4.11)
D75			0.0868
			(7.46)
IP		0.0490	0.0146
		(4.24)	(2.20)
DW	0.9307	1.3462	2.3364
Standard error of the regression	0.0233	0.0181	0.0077

Notes: (i) The additional instruments used were a fertility index, male unemployment and non-labour income.
(ii) Figures in brackets are absolute t-statistics.

considered in isolation. This is consistent with the expansion of female employment in the public sector (particularly in services) relative to the private sector (particularly in manufacturing).

How are these results changed when we consider the second model discussed above and treat relative earnings as an exogenous variable? In the first column of Table 4.3 we show the results of estimating the

Table 4.3. OLS and 2SLS estimates of demand for the whole economy (1950–80)
Dependent variable ln (relative employment)
Mean dependent variable = −0.8023

Explanatory variables	OLS			2SLS
	1	2	3	4
Constant	0.8525	0.7602	0.7133	0.4816
	(0.94)	(1.02)	(1.32)	(0.57)
$\ln(W_f/W_m)$	1.2734	−0.7743	−0.9269	−3.1043
	(5.53)	(1.89)	(2.34)	(2.40)
$\ln(I)$	0.7379	1.2405	1.2575	1.7455
	(1.18)	(2.40)	(3.41)	(2.77)
$\ln(Q/Q^*)$	0.8021	0.2634	0.2249	−0.2223
	(2.78)	(1.25)	(1.31)	(0.62)
T	−0.0027	−0.0094	−0.0096	−0.0153
	(0.76)	(3.16)	(4.21)	(3.30)
$D71$		0.0579	0.0588	0.0788
		(3.02)	(3.18)	(2.56)
$D72$		0.0098	0.0212	0.0411
		(0.43)	(1.01)	(1.20)
$D74$		0.1186	0.1141	0.1990
		(3.94)	(4.21)	(3.25)
$D75$		0.0909	0.1004	0.2470
		(2.34)	(2.61)	(2.54)
$D76$	−1.6117	−0.8696		
	(1.79)	(1.44)		
$D76 \times T$	0.0204	0.0110		
	(1.78)	(1.43)		
IP	−0.0140	0.0161	0.0001	0.0475
	(0.55)	(0.81)	(0.01)	(1.42)
DW	0.8611	1.2365	1.4663	2.4383
$\bar{R}^2$	0.8870	0.9572	0.9570	–
Standard error of the regression	0.0259	0.0159	0.0159	0.0249

Notes: (i) The additional instruments in the estimates of column (4) were a fertility index, male unemployment and non-labour income.
(ii) Figures in brackets are absolute *t*-statistics.

demand function that results from this alternative hypothesis. Now, since the only endogenous variable is relative employment, we estimate the equation with $\ln(FH/MH)$ as the dependent variable, and with $\ln(W_f/W_m)$ as one of the (exogenous) explanatory variables using ordinary least squares (OLS). Also, as discussed above, under this hypothesis the effect of the equal pay aspect of the legislation is implicit in the autonomous rise of relative wages, and any remaining shift in the demand curve must be attributed to the equal opportunities aspect of this legislation. The Sex Discrimination Act was introduced without any transitional period of adjustment and it also came into force at the end of 1975. So, instead of the set of dummies defined above, we introduce in this specification a dummy which takes the value 0 before 1976 and the value 1 afterwards ($D76$) and the interaction $D76 \times T$ to capture any accentuation of this effect as time went on.

The hypothesis does not seem to be supported by the data. The legislation effect picked up by the $D76$ and $D76 \times T$ dummies has the wrong sign (it remains negative up to 1979), and it is not statistically significant. The relative wage effect also has the wrong sign and is significant. Finally, the Durbin–Watson statistic is very low suggesting that the equation is misspecified. In fact, as we can see in column (2) of the same table, it is quite clear that the dummies representing the equal pay aspect of the legislation belong to this equation. Once they are introduced, the Durbin–Watson rises to much more satisfactory levels, the wage effect takes the right sign and is significant at the 10 per cent level, the effect of the index of industrial structure becomes larger and significant and the legislation dummies all take the expected signs. Thus, the equation in column (2) gives results which, at least qualitatively, are quite similar to those obtained in Table 4.1, which suggests that it is not correct to assume that the effect of the legislation did only operate through an increase in the price of female labour.

The main difference between these results and those in Table 4.1 concern the wage effect. Here the wage elasticity is -0.77, whereas in Table 4.1 the implied wage elasticity was -3.81. This is clearly related to the fact that in column (2) of Table 4.3 we assume that relative wages are exogenous. It would be interesting to test this exogeneity hypothesis statistically, to have an additional element of judgement as to the suitability of this model when compared to the previous one. In order to do this we exclude, in column (3), the variables ($D76$) and ($D76 \times T$), to have the same specification as that used in Table 4.1. Then in column (4), we re-estimate the equation, but this time assuming that the relative wage variable is endogenous. Thus, the equation in column (4) is the same as that in column (3) of Table 4.1, but with ln(*FH/MH*) as dependent variable and $\ln(W_f/W_m)$ as (endogenous) independent variable. The results in column (4) are, as we would expect, all consistent with those obtained previously, and the differences generated by the exogeneity assumption are clearly seen if we compare them with those in column (3).

To what extent do the data accept this exogeneity assumption? We answer this question by using the specification test proposed by Hausman (1978). Under the hypothesis that relative wages are exogenous, the OLS estimates of the parameters of the model given by column (3) are both consistent and efficient. If, on the other hand, we were to estimate the model by 2SLS (column 4), the estimates would only be consistent. Hausman shows that a test of the exogeneity assumption can be carried out by defining the statistic

$$ m = N\hat{g}'\hat{V}(\hat{g})^{-1}\hat{g} \tag{4.7} $$

where N is the number of observations, $\hat{g}$ is a vector formed by the difference between the 2SLS and the OLS estimates of the parameters of the model, and $\hat{V}(\hat{g})$ is the variance–covariance matrix associated with the variables entering vector $\hat{g}$. The statistic m is distributed asymptotically as a χ_k^2, where k is the number of estimated parameters. If m is statistically significant, then the hypothesis that the relative wages should be treated as an exogenous variable is rejected by the data.

The evaluation of expression (4.7) when comparing columns (3) and (4) is $m = 119.5$. Since m is distributed as χ_{10}^2, which has a critical value of 18.31 at the 5 per cent level, we conclude that the hypothesis that relative female wages are exogenous is rejected by the data.

Finally, we present in Table 4.4 the corresponding exercise for the private sector, as defined above. The new hypothesis is also rejected when we exclude the public sector. In this case the value of the statistic m is 102.5, which is again significant at the 5 per cent level. Other than that, the results in column (4) are all consistent with those obtained in Table 4.2 and will not be discussed further.

4.4 Summary and conclusions

In this chapter we have attempted to measure the effect of British anti-discriminatory legislation on relative levels of pay and employment. We

Table 4.4. *OLS and 2SLS estimates of demand for the private sector (1950–80)*
Dependent variable ln (relative employment)
Mean dependent variable $= -0.8046$

Explanatory variables	OLS			2SLS
	1	2	3	4
Constant	-0.6189	-0.9794	-0.3734	-1.1850
	(0.84)	(2.03)	(1.33)	(1.93)
$\ln(W_f/W_m)$	1.2637	-0.7892	-1.0803	-3.3432
	(5.91)	(1.99)	(2.68)	(2.48)
$\ln(I^*)$	-0.8845	-0.3890	0.3708	0.5589
	(1.19)	(0.78)	(1.55)	(1.43)
$\ln(Q/Q^*)$	0.8890	0.4036	0.2821	-0.0789
	(3.76)	(2.55)	(1.80)	(0.25)
T	-0.0074	-0.0108	-0.0102	-0.0132
	(6.21)	(12.01)	(12.45)	(6.48)
$D71$		0.0469	0.0580	0.0879
		(2.49)	(3.02)	(2.57)
$D72$		0.0441	0.0438	0.0634
		(1.90)	(1.99)	(1.74)
$D74$		0.0988	0.1048	0.1820
		(4.00)	(4.14)	(3.19)
$D75$		0.0983	0.1260	0.2981
		(2.59)	(3.31)	(2.74)
$D76$	-2.8106	-1.4720		
	(2.69)	(2.20)		
$D76 \times T$	0.0365	0.0194		
	(2.69)	(2.22)		
IP	-0.0182	0.0008	-0.0074	0.0430
	(0.71)	(0.04)	(0.49)	(1.21)
DW	1.2487	1.2850	1.3176	2.3185
$\bar{R}^2$	0.7380	0.9081	0.8943	–
Standard error of the regression	0.0260	0.0154	0.0165	0.0262

Notes: (i) The additional instruments in the estimates of column (4) were a fertility index, male unemployment and non-labour income.
(ii) Figures in brackets are absolute *t*-statistics.

find that even after taking into account the concomitant change of other variables, together with their interrelations within the labour market, anti-discriminatory legislation has had a positive and significant effect on both relative earnings and relative employment of women. Neither the level of economic activity, nor incomes policies, nor changes in the industrial structure, nor changes in labour supply conditions can explain alone the remarkable increase in female relative levels of pay and employment that has taken place during the seventies.

Thus, these results cannot reject the hypothesis advanced in Chapter 3. As a consequence of the legislation and of its implementation by collective agreements, employers were faced with a higher price for female labour and overall did not take any action to reduce female employment. This, in the context of our model, is captured by the increase in the relative demand curve that our estimates suggest. As a result of this increase in relative wages, which we have measured to be of about 19 per cent and which took place gradually over the first half of the seventies, there was an induced increase in relative supply, which in turn pushed down relative pay somewhat. In the end both female relative employment and female relative pay were higher than their pre-legislation levels: relative employment by more than 17 per cent and relative pay by about 15 per cent.

The estimated timing of the effects is also interesting. We have found that the effect of the legislation on relative pay was beginning to be felt as early as 1971, which is consistent with the information we have on actions directed at the implementation of equal pay by collective agreements. The main thrust, however, was concentrated in the years 1974 and 1975. It is important to emphasise that these are permanent effects. The gains attributed to incomes policies, on the other hand, are transitory and amount to less than 2 per cent. This explains quite well the shape of the evolution of relative wages in Chart 1.1. From 1970 to 1975 equal pay legislation helps to lift female wages up to around two-thirds of male wages. Then comes the effect of incomes policies causing the bulge observed in the years 1976 and 1977, which quickly disappears due to the temporary nature of these policies. After 1978, with the influence of incomes policies gone, relative pay stabilises itself around the two-thirds level achieved in 1975.

These results, we have also found, are likely to be quite general. The substantial increase in both relative pay and employment cannot be explained on the basis of the possible non-cost-minimising behaviour of the public sector. Although it is true that during the period considered female employment in the public sector expanded at a faster rate than in the private sector, we have not been able to identify any difference of substance between the two sectors concerning the effect of equal pay legislation.

5

The extent of sex discrimination in Great Britain

A. ZABALZA and J.L. ARRUFAT

The isolated effect of equal pay legislation on female relative wages has been estimated at around 19 per cent. Is this a large or a small effect? Can we conclude from such evidence that the legislation has been successful? To answer these questions we need to measure the extent of discrimination. That is, the differential in wages between men and women that cannot be explained on the basis of differences in productive capacity. This should give us an approximate idea of the maximum effect that the legislation could possibly have. Even if it had been completely successful, sex wage differentials would still remain if productive characteristics of men and women were different. So, a situation in which sex discrimination had been eliminated would not normally be a situation in which female wages were equal. The purpose of this chapter is to find out what is the wage differential that would exist with no discrimination, and therefore to evaluate the extent to which equal pay has approached this goal.

However, the measurement of sex discrimination is a difficult task. It has long been recognised that the presence of wage differentials between men and women is neither necessary nor sufficient for discrimination to exist. Different wage rates for men and women of different levels of productivity do not constitute evidence of discrimination. Equal wage rates for men and women of different levels of productivity do suggest discriminatory practices. Thus economists, in their attempts to measure the extent of discrimination, have been careful to take into account variations in productivity when comparing wage rates.

The problem with this procedure is that many of the differences in productivity traits may be themselves the result of discrimination. Even if the whole of the sex wage differential could be attributed to differences in education between men and women, it would be impossible to ascertain that discrimination did not exist. Women might choose less education than

70

men if they expect a lower return on their investment, or less opportunities to use their skills. The response of economists to this difficulty has been to step their analysis one level down. Instead of measuring the extent of discrimination, they have limited themselves to measuring the extent to which equal productivity traits are paid differently in the market; what has come to be known as discrimination in the market. But it is important to emphasise that this narrowing down of the concept of discrimination does not by itself solve all the problems. The measurement of productive traits is also a difficult task, and the proxies that economists are forced to use may be poor and scarce. Despite these difficulties, this chapter attempts to measure the extent of the wage differential between married men and women attributable to market discrimination using data from the *General Household Survey* for 1975.

A previous analysis of these data by Greenhalgh (1980) concentrated mostly on the wage differential between men and single women. This was done as an attempt to control for the different supply behaviour between married and single women, and it also allowed the author to obtain an estimate of discrimination which was not affected by the limited information that GHS data give on work experience for married women. The nearest thing that can be ascertained is the time period that has elapsed since a woman left school, and for married women this is likely to be a very bad proxy for experience. Also, it has been shown with other data by Mincer and Polachek (1974) that interruptions in participation have a significant negative effect on women's wage prospects. Therefore, results on the wage differential between married men and married women are bound to be of little value unless this problem is first taken into account, and this is why most analyses have concentrated on single women to carry out the comparison. Married women, however, constitute an increasingly important segment of the female working population and it would be interesting to understand, at least partially, the factors that may explain their low pay relative to married men.

In this chapter we propose a method which can help in carrying out such analysis. As far as experience is concerned, there are at least two problems with the conventional analysis of wages of married women: one of measurement and another of endogeneity. The measurement problem has already been discussed, and refers to the inadequacy of the data to provide information on actual work experience. But even if such information was available, it is incorrect to assume that work experience is independent of the level of wages that a woman can command in the market. This issue has been extensively considered in labour supply studies, but rather neglected in the study of earnings functions (for notable exceptions see Blinder (1973) and Mincer and Polachek (1974)). The method that we propose here deals with both problems by making use of a labour supply model which enables us to predict actual experience of married women in terms of exogenous variables concerning her and her family.

Naturally, experience is not the only endogenous variable normally used in wage equations. Education is another important determinant of earnings capacity which should also be considered endogenous. The number of children, although not normally used as a direct determinant of earnings, has an important influence on the wife's market experience and is also likely to be influenced by family earnings. In our analysis we will treat these variables as exogenous. This is likely to bias our results, although we believe that the extent of this bias is much smaller than that originated from the exogenous treatment of experience. Our only excuse for not doing better is that we know very little about the way in which earnings capacity may influence education and fertility decisions.

A final question that our analysis considers, also somewhat neglected in previous earnings studies, is the possible bias caused by ignoring the truncated nature of the sample on which female wages are estimated. Since the participation decision also depends on the variables on which the wage equation is defined, we may be using for our comparison analysis the earnings capacity of a group of women which is not representative of that of the total female population. Our results suggest that these problems are empirically important, and that ignoring them may lead to a substantial overestimation of the extent of discrimination between married men and married women.

In the first section of this chapter we present the theoretical model underlying our analysis. In the second the data are briefly discussed, in the third we estimate the wage equations and in the fourth the extent of discrimination is evaluated. The fifth and last section summarises the chapter and presents the conclusions.

5.1 Theoretical framework

The usual strategy to measure discrimination (Oxaca, 1973) consists in specifying a wage equation for each of the groups under consideration which is defined over a set of personal attributes thought to represent, or to be correlated with, productivity in the market. If we index men by m and women by f, two such equations could be

$$\ln(W_m) = \alpha X_m \tag{5.1}$$

$$\ln(W_f) = \beta X_f \tag{5.2}$$

where W_i and X_i ($i = $ m, f) are the hourly wage and the set of personal characteristics of each group respectively. Men's attributes are paid by the market according to the set of coefficients α and those of women according to β. For a given set of characteristics, the (logarithm of the) relative wage $\ln(W_m) - \ln(W_f)$ can be decomposed in a part which is attributable to different endowments of attributes and a part which is attributable to different market returns to a given endowment. From (5.1) and (5.2) we have

$$\ln(W_m) - \ln(W_f) = \alpha(X_m - X_f) + X_f(\alpha - \beta) \tag{5.3}$$

Expression (5.3) measures the logarithm of the relative wage (which equals the logarithim of $(1 + D)$, where D is the relative differential in wages $(W_m - W_f)/W_f$) as the sum of two components. The first, $\alpha(X_m - X_f)$, measures that part of the relative wage which would persist even if productive attributes were paid the same to men and women. The second, $X_f(\alpha - \beta)$, measures that part of the relative wage which would be observed if equal endowments for men and women were paid differently by the market, and is the portion of the relative wage usually attributed to discrimination.[25]

One of the variables normally included in the set X is market experience, which is generally associated with higher wages and presumably reflects the higher level of post-school training accumulated by people with more time in the market. As far as married women are concerned, there are three problems with the procedure outlined above, all of them connected directly or indirectly with that variable: one of measurement, another of endogeneity and a last one of selectivity.

Married women typically experience breaks in their labour force participation, and most cross-sectional sets of data do not give information either on the amount of time spent outside the labour market or on the timing of these breaks. Thus economists are forced to use proxies, such as the amount of potential experience estimated from age and educational level, which not only are very poor measures of the amount of time women have spent in the labour force but also, and most importantly, may fail to capture the sample variation in actual experience. Studies done with cross-sectional data in which this information was available (Malkiel and Malkiel, 1973) or with longitudinal data (Mincer and Polachek, 1974) suggest that the estimated return to experience is seriously biased downwards when the incorrect measure is used.

Even if detailed information on labour market experience was available, this variable should not be considered exogenous. Experience is made up of accumulated participation, and participation depends, among other factors, on wage rates. For men this is probably not very important, given that most men participate continuously irrespective of the level of wages they can command.[26] But for married women, the strong wage elasticity usually found for participation, might seriously bias the coefficient on experience if (5.2) was estimated by OLS. The point that (5.2) should be considered as only one equation of a more extensive economic model has been previously made by Blinder (1973), and the extent to which this endogeneity problem may be important is documented with US data by Mincer and Polachek (1978).

The final problem is that to estimate (5.2) we can only use a self-selected sample (women who work in the market) in which the rule of selection depends also on wages. The bias generated by this selectivity process has been extensively studied by Heckman (1979) but only recently has this started being taken into account in discrimination studies.[27] If selectivity bias is important, this may give a distorted picture of the extent of discrimination. Women who participate are not necessarily representative of the whole population of married women and, in principle, we are interested in the wage structure that the market potentially offers to the whole female population (participants and non-participants). Taking the truncation of the sample into account should produce estimates which reflect better this potential wage structure than those obtained on the basis of only working women.

The procedure that we propose in this paper attempts to solve these three problems by interpreting (5.2) as only one equation of an extended model of labour supply. Roughly speaking, we solve the measurement problem by projecting backwards the probability of participation of each woman in turn. Although this does not give us the timing or the number of breaks that may have occurred, it produces an estimate of the *overall* amount of time spent in the labour market and, therefore, also an estimate of the *overall* amount of time spent at home. Clearly, direct information on actual experience is always preferable, but in its absence our procedure provides a reasonable way of improving on the potential experience proxy that one is forced to use with most bodies of cross-sectional data. The labour supply model is specified so that the participation decision can be predicted on the basis of variables which, within the context of the present problem, can be taken as exogenous. Thus the problem of endogeneity does not arise since the relationship between actual experience and the exogenous variables of the model is taken into account. Finally, the selectivity problem is dealt with by using the estimated probability of participation to correct equation (5.2) for truncation, following Heckman's (1979) method.

The participation model is more fully described in a previous work by one of the authors (Zabalza, 1983). Among other things, that model predicts the individual probability of participation as the cumulative of a unit normal deviate Z_i, which is defined on a linear function of a vector of economic variables and personal and family characteristics. In particular

$$P_i = 1 - F(Z_i) \tag{5.4}$$

where

$$Z_i = \gamma(\ln(y_i), \ln(w_i), \mathbf{Q}_i, \mathbf{S}_i) \tag{5.5}$$

and where P is the probability of participation, $F(\cdot)$ is the cumulative function of the standardised normal distribution, y is the family net income when the wife does not participate (that is, it includes the family unearned income and the husband's net earnings), w is the predicted wife's gross wage, $\mathbf{Q}_i$ is a vector of characteristics which includes the number of children by age groups and the age of the wife, $\mathbf{S}_i$ a vector of characteristics which includes race and health dummies, and $\gamma(\cdot)$ is a linear function.

The wife's wage is predicted in turn by a linear function $\phi(\cdot)$ which relates the logarithm of the wage to the age of the wife (a group of four age dummies which we will denote by $\mathbf{A}_i$) and to a vector of personal and family characteristics $\mathbf{R}_i$, which includes education, father's occupation, race and health

$$\ln(w_i) = \phi(\mathbf{A}_i, \mathbf{R}_i) \tag{5.6}$$

Although equation (5.6) already gives an estimate of the determinants of the female wage structure, it is not the wage equation in which we are interested. It should be interpreted as a first-round estimate of wages whose only purpose is to predict the probability of participation and, thus, help us to specify the better equation (5.2).

Equations (5.4) to (5.6) constitute a labour supply model which can be used to estimate the probability of participation corresponding to the period of time to which the data belong. But the model can also provide information regarding past participation probabilities and, therefore, help to estimate accumulated labour market experience. If the vector Z_i could be projected backwards to the age at which the woman in question left school, we could obtain an estimate of market experience by integrating these past predicted probabilities of experience. Take the time dimension to be one year, and define P_{it} as the probability that the ith woman participates during the year t, which is made to depend on the index Z_{it} according to (5.4), where Z_{it} is the vector (5.5) defined for the values that the independent variables take at year t. We have that

$$P_{iT} = 1 - F(Z_{iT})$$

where T is the year in which the model (5.4) to (5.6) is estimated. Then, accumulated market experience X_i can be defined as

$$X_i = \sum_{j=0}^{E_i - 1} P_{i, T-j} \tag{5.7}$$

where E_i is the number of years that have elapsed since the ith woman left school (i.e. potential experience). Also, we can define accumulated time outside the market H_i as

$$H_i = E_i - X_i \tag{5.8}$$

Expressions (5.7) and (5.8) give us then the variables that should enter (5.2) instead of potential experience. X_i because it is a more accurate measure of accumulated market experience and thus of post-school training (Mincer, 1974), and H_i because time at home may depreciate the market skills acquired by the individual (Mincer and Polachek, 1974). The question then remains, how to predict the different values of P_{it}?

The model contains two types of variables. Dated variables which will change each year and fixed attributes which remain unaltered through the period under consideration. The latter are included in the vectors S_i and R_i. Thus, race and health (the variables included in S) are supposed not to change during the period that goes from the present to the year in which the woman left school. This is an unquestionable assumption as far as race is concerned but somewhat dubious for health; however, since there is little variation in the sample concerning this variable and since its effect on participation is small, we do not believe this assumption alters our results much. The vector **R** includes, in addition to race and health, education, which by definition is given since the period under consideration goes back to the date the woman left school, and father's occupation which again seems reasonable to treat as a fixed attribute.

The rest of the variables all change over time and this needs to be taken into account in order to predict P_{it} correctly. The vector **Q** includes seven variables for the number of children by age groups. To find out the value that each variable takes when we go back in time involves some tedious manipulations of the data set, but is just a matter of arithmetic. The same applies to the four variables for age that complete the vector **T** and that also form the vector **A** of the wage equation.

To predict backwards the woman's wage w_i we simply use equation (5.6) under the assumptions just discussed. For other family income y_i, however, we do not have any such equation since this variable is available for all families for the estimation year. Since the largest part of this variable is made up of husband's net earnings, we predict the rate of change from year to year by means of an equation run on the husband's age, education and occupation. The specification of this function $\pi(\cdot)$ that best fitted the data allows the age effect to vary depending on the educational level of the individual, although simpler specifications produced very similar results. We denote this function as

$$\ln(y_i) = \pi(XA_i, (XA_i)^2, \mathbf{X}S_i, XA_i\,\mathbf{X}S_i, (XA_i)^2\,\mathbf{X}S_i, \mathbf{X}O) \quad (5.9)$$

where XA_i is age of the husband, $\mathbf{X}S_i$ is a set of two educational dummies for the husband and $\mathbf{X}O$ is a set of occupational dummies. In using (5.9) to project $\ln(y_i)$ backwards, we assume that $\mathbf{X}S$ and $\mathbf{X}O$ are fixed attributes and that only the husband's age changes. Then *for each year* of the period considered we calculate the rate of change of predicted family income and apply these rates recursively to actual net family income. Thus, $\ln(y_{T-1})$, the logarithm of net family income one period before the estimation year, is defined as

$$\ln(y_{T-1}) = \ln(y_T) + \ln(\hat{y}_{T-1}) - \ln(\hat{y}_T) \quad (5.10)$$

where $\ln(y_T)$ is the logarithm of actual net family income and $\ln(\hat{y}_{T-1})$ and $\ln(\hat{y}_T)$ are predicted terms using (5.9). For j periods back, (5.10) would read

$$\ln(y_{T-j}) = \ln(y_{T-j+1}) + \ln(\hat{y}_{T-j}) - \ln(\hat{y}_{T-j+1})$$
$$= \ln(y_T) + \ln(\hat{y}_{T-j}) - \ln(\hat{y}_T)$$

Using this method we can predict back female wages and other family income, but this prediction will be in terms of the real purchasing power of money in 1975. Since real wages have increase, this would lead to a substantial overestimation of wages and family income when going back in time. We therefore adjust the estimated female wages and family income according to the evolution of real earnings in Britain since 1930 (see Annex to this chapter for the indices of real earnings used and for the method of adjustment followed).

The procedure just outlined enables us to predict P_{it} and therefore X_i and H_i using, in addition to fixed attributes, only the time evolution of age and family composition. It does in fact treat most of the variables of interest as endogenously determined by the model, with the exception of family composition which, although treated as given, is to a certain extent determined endogenously. Given the fact that we know much less about fertility than about participation, we maintain this assumption as the only option open to use. The bias that this may cause is probably much smaller than that which would be caused by ignoring the endogeneity of participation.[28]

Another variable which is maintained fixed, but which does not appear explicitly in the analysis, is marital status. The model (5.4) to (5.6) is estimated for married couples and, therefore, does not necessarily reflect the behavioural parameters of single women. This means that when we go back in our projection, the probability of participation is always predicted under the assumption that the woman in question is married, while it is obvious that a large proportion of women must be single for some of the initial years of the period considered. Again, since there is no information on marriage dates, there is little we can do about this. We note, however, that the problem is bound to be small because the labour supply model, even if estimated in married families, predicts participation probabilities very near to one for young couples with no children.

These probabilities of participation will reflect labour supply behaviour as estimated in 1975; but this behaviour may have changed over time for reasons other than those related to changes in economic circumstances or to personal and family characteristics. When using longitudinal data (Joshi *et al.*, 1981), it has been found that economic and demographic variables were only able to explain part of the increase in female participation over time, and that significant unexplained cohort effects remained. Therefore, we need to take these effects into account when predicting backwards the probabilities of participation.[29] This involves adjusting the predicted participation possibilities by factors related to the age cohort to which each woman belongs. The estimated parameters for 1975 reflect the average behaviour of women of different ages. If cohort effects have increased participation over time, these parameters will underestimate the participation probabilities of younger women, and overestimate those of older women. These adjustment factors then weight the predicted probabilities so that, while maintaining the average (in order to reproduce the behaviour of 1975), they increase the probabilities of younger women and decrease those of older women (see the Annex to this chapter for the method followed to calculate these weighting factors).

This completes the procedure that we propose to deal with the first two issues mentioned above: the measurement and the endogeneity problems. The third problem is tackled using Heckman's two-step method in order to correct for selectivity bias (Heckman, 1979). The problem arises because the wage equation can only be estimated on a sample of participants, since it is only for participant women that we have observations on wages. If the group of participants was a random subsample of the total population of married women, there would exist no problem; estimating (5.2) by OLS on the subsample of participants should produce unbiased estimates of β. However, if the subsample of participants is not random (i.e. if the decision to participate is related to the variables of the equation) then OLS estimation of (5.2), only on participants, will produce biased estimates of β. Heckman shows that this bias can be corrected if an additional regressor,, related to the probability of participation, is included in (5.2). This new regressor λ is defined as

$$\lambda_i = \frac{f(Z_i)}{1 - F(Z_i)} \tag{5.11}$$

where $F(\cdot)$ and Z_i have already been defined, and $f(\cdot)$ is the density function of the standard normal distribution. Since from (5.5) we know Z_i for each woman in the sample, λ_i can be calculated for each participant and included as a regressor in (5.2). We turn now to the empirical results, but first we discuss the data and the specification of equations (5.1) and (5.2).

5.2 Data and specification of wage equations

The analysis is based on the 1975 General Household Survey, using data on 3984 families in which the husband was less than 65 years old, working and not self-employed, and the wife was less than 60 years old and not self-employed. The number of families with working wife was 2335 which gives a participation rate of 58.61 per cent. Using the 1975 GHS data enables us to produce results complementary to those presented by Greenhalgh (1980), who also uses these data but concentrates mainly on the wage comparison between single women and men.

The variables used in the auxiliary labour supply model have already been introduced in the previous section. We concentrate here on the variables that will be included in the specification of the wage equations (5.1) and (5.2). Frequently these equations are explicitly based on the human capital framework of Becker (1964) and Mincer (1974), but this is not the only story that can be attached to the correlation between earnings capacity and certain personal attributes. In fact, as Blinder (1976) points out, Mincer's model is a theory about earnings and here we are interested in wages rather than in the product of wages and labour supply. Therefore in specifying (5.1) and (5.2) we will adopt a rather agnostic attitude about the process that links wages and personal characteristics, and simply take these wage equations as useful devices to hold constant certain characteristics in order to make comparisons between groups of workers as homogeneous as possible.

This, of course, needs to be qualified. If our purpose was only to obtain homogeneity, we could use quite a large set of standardising variables. But our purpose is to measure discrimination and this may take the form not only of different pay for equal attributes but also of different distributions of attributes within the groups under comparison. A case in point is the inclusion of occupational or industrial variables in the set **X**. Clearly, one of the possible channels through which discrimination can operate is the restriction of entry to certain occupations. If this was the case, including occupational variables in **X** might result in more standardisation than needed, since part of the differential attributed to different characteristics would in fact be due to discrimination in the form of unequal employment opportunities.

Does that mean that occupational or industrial variables should be excluded from **X**? As with practically everything concerning the measurement of discrimination, it is difficult to give a definite answer to this question. To the extent that women suffer restrictions to entry in some occupations, standardising for occupations may understate the extent of discrimination. But to the extent that the occupational wage structure reflects compensating differentials, ignoring the occupational and industrial distribution may lead to an exaggeration of the extent of discrimination.

As many other authors have done, we will adopt a rather eclectic position and present two sets of results. One in which we consider the simplest specification consistent with the human capital framework and include in **X** only education and experience variables; and another in which, in addition to these basic productivity traits, we also standardise for the occupational and industrial distributions, and for two other variables which, although important in other studies, are not very significant in the present context (race and health). The two specifications can be thought of as providing the range of the extent of discrimination, with the former giving an upper limit and the latter a lower limit to this range.

The variables used to estimate equations (5.1) and (5.2) are as follows:

(i) *Wages* The dependent variable is the natural logarithm of hourly earnings and is obtained by dividing annual earnings by hours. As Greenhalgh (1980) notes, this leads to a slightly inflated estimate of the basic wage rate, particularly for men undertaking overtime work, but the error is small and can be safely ignored. Table 5.1, which presents the mean and standard deviations of some of the variables used to estimate (5.1) and (5.2), shows, as expected, that the average wage for married men is larger than that for married women. Women's wages are on average only 62.3 per cent of those of men.

(ii) *Education* To allow for the possible non-linear effect of education on wages we divide the years of schooling into three spline variables. The first measures the years of education up to 11 years, the second measures the number of additional years of education beyond 11 and up to 13 years, and the third measures the number of additional years of education beyond 13 years. As the second row of Table 1 indicates, although men have more education than women the difference is very small. The splines show that this difference is practically non-existent as far as primary education is concerned, but widens somewhat for higher education levels.

(iii) *Experience* The first experience variable we use is 'potential experience' which is defined as age minus school leaving age. Here again the difference between men and women is very small, but this just reflects the underlying distributions in age and schooling between the two groups. The

Table 5.1. *Mean and standard deviation of basic variables used to estimate equations (5.1) and (5.2)*
Married men and married women GHS 1975

	Men		Women	
Variable	Mean	Standard deviation	Mean	Standard deviation
ln(wage)	0.284	0.413	−0.190	0.435
Years of schooling	10.960	1.976	10.754	1.578
Years of schooling (up to 11)	10.307	0.461	10.293	0.455
Years of schooling (beyond 11 and up to 13)	0.307	0.690	0.260	0.629
Years of schooling (beyond 13)	0.347	1.064	0.224	0.829
Potential experience	24.454	11.907	23.154	11.264
Actual experience	24.454	11.907	15.958	8.378
Home time	—	—	7.196	4.032
Non-white	0.018	0.133	0.017	0.130
Poor health	0.221	0.415	0.196	0.397
Sample	3984		2335	
Participation rate	1.000		0.586	
Observed relative wage (W_f/W_m)		0.623		

second is the estimate of 'actual experience' that we obtain using the procedure discussed in Section 5.2. For men this is the same as 'potential experience' but, as expected, for women it is much smaller. Also, the estimate shows that the coefficient of variation of 'actual experience' is higher than that of 'potential experience' (52.5 per cent as opposed to 48.6 per cent). Thus the procedure does not correct uniformly the value of potential experience but introduces variation which is attributable to the way in which exogenous factors affect differently the participation decisions of women across the sample. The third experience variable we use is 'home time', which is simply defined as 'potential experience' minus 'actual experience' and which ought to have a negative effect on wages if depression effects of non-participation are important.

It is interesting to note that the estimates that we obtain for the variables 'actual experience' and 'home time' are very close to the values obtained in Stewart and Greenhalgh (1982) from the only retrospective longitudinal data set available in the UK. Using the *National Training Survey*, they calculate that for women who were working in 1975, the average number of years of participation is 14.7 (which compares with our 15.9 figure), and the average number of years of non-participation is 6.7 (which compares with our 7.2 figure). If we look at this comparison in relative terms, the similarity is even more remarkable. Their sample (which includes also single women) is younger than ours and therefore has a lower mean for years of potential experience (21.4 as opposed to 23.2). Relative to this total, actual experience represents 68.7 per cent in their case 68.9, per cent in ours, and home time 31.3 per cent in their case and 31.1 per cent in ours. Given the different data sets involved, the closeness of these results is reassuring and suggests that our procedure does indeed manage to measure the actual amount of time that women work in the market.

(iv) *Non-white* One dummy variable which takes the value 1 for non-white individuals and 0 otherwise.

(v) *Poor health* One dummy variable which takes the value 1 if the individual has a long-standing illness and 0 otherwise.

(vi) *Occupational distribution* Eleven dummy variables were used for occupational groups. Table 5.2 gives details of the distribution of men and women across occupations. Consistently with other data referring to

Table 5.2. Occupational distribution of married men and married women GHS 1975 (per cent)

Occupation	Men	Women
1. Professional	5.31	0.56
2. Manager (large establishment)	9.36	1.24
3. Manager (small establishment)	4.84	1.11
4. Non-manual (intermediate)	7.33	13.88
5. Non-manual (junior)	10.37	38.84
6. Manual (supervisory)	7.51	1.20
7. Manual (skilled)	34.66	5.14
8. Manual (semi-skilled)	16.42	15.33
9. Personal service worker	0.48	13.02
10. Manual (unskilled)	2.59	9.68
11. Armed forces	1.13	–
All	100	100

Table 5.3. Industrial distribution of married men and women,
GHS 1975 (per cent)

Industry	Men	Women
1. Agriculture	1.05	0.77
2. Mining	3.51	0.09
3. Food	3.09	2.61
4. Coal and oil	0.45	0.09
5. Chemicals	2.61	1.67
6. Metals	3.66	0.90
7. Engineering	19.48	9.42
8. Instruments	0.73	0.56
9. Shipbuilding	1.96	0.26
10. Textiles	2.03	2.18
11. Leather	0.25	0.30
12. Clothing	0.63	3.77
13. Bricks, etc.	2.61	1.24
14. Timber	1.10	0.47
15. Paper	2.94	1.93
16. Other manufacturing	1.63	1.31
17. Construction	10.97	0.94
18. Utilities	2.74	0.86
19. Transport	9.16	3.00
20. Distribution	7.38	16.40
21. Finance	4.27	5.10
22. Professional and scientific	6.48	25.70
23. Miscellaneous services	4.14	14.82
24. Public administration and defence	7.13	5.61
All	100	100

all women (e.g. *New Earnings Survey* data), there is a substantial degree of
sex segregation in the case of married women, 54 per cent of the female
labour force are concentrated in two occupations, non-manual (junior)
and manual (semi-skilled), which only employ 26 per cent of the male
labour force. Looking at the question from the other end, we see that the
first two occupations in terms of male employment, manual (skilled) and
manual (semi-skilled), employ 51 per cent of married men and only
20 per cent of married women.

   (vii) *Industrial distribution* Twenty-four dummy variables were used for
industrial sectors. Table 5.3 presents the male and female distributions
across these 24 sectors and again suggests a fairly high degree of segregation.

The first three industrial sectors in terms of female employment – professional and scientific (mainly school teachers), distribution and miscellaneous services – employ almost 57 per cent of the total working population of married women and only 18 per cent of the working population of married men.

5.3 The effect of actual experience and home time on wages

The labour supply model specified in equations (5.4) to (5.6) is largely auxiliary in the context of this paper. Its only use here is to help to measure more correctly the accumulated actual experience of the wife and the length of time spent outside the labour force. Thus, we relegate the results of its estimation to the Annex to this chapter. A more detailed explanation of the model and an analysis of the results obtained can be found in Zabalza (1983). Here we want to concentrate on the comparison of the wage structures represented by equations (5.1) and (5.2), and on the difference that dealing with the problems of measurement, endogeneity and selectivity may make to the evaluation of sexual discrimination.

Table 5.4 presents the results of estimating the wage equations, using only education and experience variables. Education is entered by means of three spline variables, as discussed above, and experience is entered with both linear and quadratic terms to capture the non-linear effect of this variable on wages. Column (1) reports the results for the male wage equation and the other three columns refer to different specifications of the female equation. In column (2) we report the results of using 'potential experience' as the relevant experience variable, in column (3) the measurement and endogeneity problems are dealt with by entering 'actual experience' and 'home time' instead of 'potential experience'. Finally, column (4) reports the results obtained when the last specification is corrected for selectivity bias.

The results obtained with 'potential experience' (columns 1 and 2) are similar to those of other authors. The return to primary education is larger for males, but the marginal effect of additional years of schooling (secondary and higher education) is larger for females. For males, there is a clear break in the rates of return after primary education while for women the relationship is practically linear throughout the whole schooling period. As far as experience is concerned, the conclusion that the wage profile of married women is fairly flat is substantiated by the present data. While the

Table 5.4. Wage equations for married men and married women
GHS 1975, dependent variable ln (hourly earnings)

Independent variable	Men	Women		
	(1)	(2)	(3)	(4)
Constant	− 3.007	− 1.658	− 1.689	− 1.854
	(16.686)	(6.573)	(6.931)	(7.678)
Years of schooling	0.282	0.132	0.128	0.127
(up to 11)	(16.395)	(5.488)	(5.511)	(5.522)
Years of schooling	0.058	0.085	0.107	0.108
(beyond 11 and up to 13)	(3.494)	(3.696)	(4.775)	(4.863)
Years of schooling	0.056	0.126	0.119	0.125
(beyond 13)	(6.154)	(8.485)	(8.269)	(8.805)
Potential experience	0.029	0.006		
	(12.609)	(1.790)		
(Potential experience)^2	− 0.0005	− 0.0001		
	(11.114)	(1.714)		
Actual experience			0.036	0.051
			(6.848)	(9.208)
(Actual experience)^2			− 0.00066	− 0.00098
			(4.496)	(6.502)
Home time			− 0.032	− 0.050
			(4.554)	(6.824)
(Home time)^2			0.00010	0.00044
			(0.241)	(1.022)
λ				0.248
				(7.870)
$\bar{R}^2$	0.214	0.179	0.244	0.263
N	3984	2335	2315	2315

Note: Figures in parentheses are *t*-values.

men's profile increases at a rate of 3 per cent per year of experience, the coefficient on women's 'potential experience' indicates a rate of growth substantially less than 1 per cent and is only significant at the 10 per cent level.[30]

Does it follow, however, from these results that married women's experience is rewarded to such a small extent by the market? Our findings in column (3) clearly suggest that this is not the case. When 'potential experience' is divided up into 'actual experience' and 'home time', we see that the lack of slope in the observed wage profile of married women was the result of compounding into one effect the positive influence of actual experience and the negative influence of non-participation on wages. When these two effects are disentangled the conclusions that we obtain are very different. The labour market does reward actual experience of married women about the same as that of married men (in fact, the point estimate of women is slightly higher than that of men), but the depreciation effect of non-participation on wages is of an equivalent magnitude. The loss in earnings capacity that a married woman experiences for each year that she stays at home is almost as large as the growth in earnings that she would obtain if she participated. As in the case of men, the effect of 'actual experience' takes a well-defined quadratic shape, but the negative effect of non-participation is practically linear. Another feature of the coefficients in column (3) is that while the results on experience are very different, those on education remain similar to those obtained in column (2).

These results are somewhat different from previous ones based on British data (see, for instance, Greenhalgh (1980)), but not inconsistent with US studies estimated on longitudinal data (Mincer and Polachek, 1974, 1978). As with the present results, measuring market experience correctly and taking care of its endogeneity substantially raises the effect of experience on wages. Also, the specification more comparable to ours in Mincer and Polachek (1978) gives a depreciation effect which is very similar in absolute magnitude to the positive effect of actual experience.

Another piece of consistent evidence is that given by Malkiel and Malkiel (1973); when they measure experience as 'potential experience' the male coefficient is larger than the female coefficient (0.044 as compared to 0.037), but when they use actual experience (which they obtain directly from information in their data set) the return to experience becomes larger for females than for males (0.059 as compared to 0.054). That is precisely the sort of effect that we detect in our exercise. We believe that this independent evidence, together with the dramatic improvement that the new variables have on the performance of the wage equation (the adjusted R^2 increases from 0.18 to 0.24 in a sample of more than 2000 observations), lends support to our method of dealing with the measurement and endogeneity problems, and suggests that these are more important than previously thought.

The last column of Table 5.4 presents the estimated equation corrected for selectivity bias. The results are again quite remarkable. Selectivity bias has proved in the past a very insignificant problem in the case of British data. In previous work with predicted wages in terms of age (or potential experience) the coefficient on λ has usually been insignificant and the inclusion of this variable as a regressor has made little difference to the effect of education or experience. When market experience is correctly measured, on the other hand, things take an altogether different turn. The education coefficients are practically unaltered but the coefficients on 'market experience' and 'home time' increase substantially both in absolute value and level of significance. The return on female market experience is definitely greater than that obtained by men (in fact, it is comparable to the estimate obtained in the Malkiel and Malkiel study: 0.051 here as compared with 0.059 in their case), but there is also a substantial increase in the depreciation effect. Again participation and non-participation appear to influence wages similarly but with opposite sign. Also, the result has its parallel in US literature; Heckman (1977) finds that selectivity bias becomes detectable only when the endogenous nature of accumulated market experience is taken into account.[31]

Table 5.5 presents the results of standardising the wage equations for the occupational and industrial distribution, plus health and race. The detailed regressions are presented in the Annex to this chapter and here we concentrate only on the education and experience variables. As expected, the return to schooling goes down somewhat, since it will now be captured by the effect of the occupational and industrial dummies, and the constant term is now both nearer to zero and more similar between men and women, due to the greater extent of standardisation. Other than that, all the results concerning experience remain unchanged and will not be discussed further.

5.4 The measurement of discrimination

How do the results reported in Section 5.4 affect our conclusions on the extent of discrimination? We would like to stress again the thin foundations on which this measurement has to be based. As in the case of other analyses, all we can do is to attempt the identification of certain factors which are related to the observed differentials in wages between married men and women, and attribute the unexplained residual to market discrimination.[32] All that we have done above is to attempt a more correct measurement of some of these factors (market experience), and to include in the analysis new variables which appear to be strongly correlated with female wages (home time).

Table 5.5. Wage equations for married men and married women
Extended set of standardising variables, GHS 1975
Dependent variable ln (hourly earnings)

Independent variable	Men	Women		
	(1)	(2)	(3)	(4)
Constant	− 0.919	− 0.707	− 0.870	− 1.067
	(5.152)	(2.525)	(3.171)	(3.195)
Years of schooling	0.138	0.046	0.052	0.051
(up to 11)	(8.571)	(2.000)	(2.274)	(2.268)
Years of schooling	0.013	0.033	0.054	0.056
(beyond 11 and up to 13)	(0.884)	(1.500)	(2.525)	(2.636)
Years of schooling	0.032	0.106	0.097	0.105
(beyond 13)	(3.877)	(7.114)	(6.666)	(7.314)
Potential experience	0.021	0.007		
	(10.144)	(2.258)		
(Potential experience)^2	− 0.0004	− 0.0001		
	(9.535)	(2.027)		
Actual experience			0.030	0.044
			(6.062)	(8.293)
(Actual experience)^2			− 0.00055	− 0.00084
			(3.921)	(5.826)
Home time			− 0.024	− 0.040
			(3.595)	(5.754)
(Home time)^2			− 0.00025	0.00027
			(0.614)	(0.663)
λ				0.222
				(7.383)
$\bar{R}^2$	0.395	0.295	0.335	0.350
N	3984	2335	2315	2315

Notes: (i) Figures in parentheses are t-values.
(ii) In addition to the variables shown the equations include 10 dummies for occupational categories, 23 dummies for industries, 1 dummy for health and 1 dummy for race.

We measure the residual following the method outlined in Section 5.1. The decomposition is based on equation (5.3), but we also identify as a separate component that part of the logarithmic gap between male and female wages which is explained by the depreciation effect of non-participation. If we denote the 'home time' variables by the vector $\mathbf{H}_i (i = m, f)$, and the corresponding coefficients by $\boldsymbol{\alpha}_h$ (male coefficients) and $\boldsymbol{\beta}_h$ (female coefficients), then expression (5.3) would read

$$\ln(W_m) - \ln(W_f) = \alpha(X_m - X_f) + \alpha_h(H_m - H_f)$$
$$+ H_f(\alpha_h - \beta_h) + X_f(\alpha - \beta)$$

which, since by definition $\alpha_h = 0$, reduces to

$$\ln(W_m) - \ln(W_f) = \alpha(X_m - X_f) - H_f\beta_h + X_f(\alpha - \beta) \qquad (5.12)$$

As before, the first term on the right-hand side corresponds to that part of the logarithmic gap between wages explained by differences in endowments, the second is that part of the gap due to the depreciation of non-participation by married women, and the last is the unexplained residual.

Table 5.6 evaluates expression (5.12) and reports each of its components in terms of percentages. The first three rows correspond to the wage equation specified only on education and experience variables (Table 5.4), while the specification used in the last three rows includes in addition ten dummies for occupational groups, 23 dummies for industrial sectors, one dummy for race and another for health (Table 5.5). The three comparisons made correspond to each of the variants tried for the female wage equation. The first comparison uses the wage equation for married women in which experience is measured simply by means of age minus school leaving age (i.e., 'potential experience'), and corresponds to the specification most frequently used in discrimination studies. According to this comparison only a very small part of the gap would be explained by differences in endowments (2.7 per cent), the rest — practically the whole of the differential (97.3 per cent) — being attributed to market discrimination. Correspondingly, the differential between male and female wages that would be justified is very small. If discrimination were eliminated, married female wages would be as high as 98.7 per cent of married male wages (last column of Table 5.6), while in fact they were (in 1975) 62.3 per cent.

These results are clearly exaggerated due to the way in which market experience has been measured in the second column. In that specification married women are supposed to have almost as much market experience as men, and thus (given the also similar level of education that both sexes have) the small part of the gap accounted for by differences in attributes. However, when market experience is correctly measured, and when its endogenous nature is taken into account, differences in attributes become much more important and explain more than 11 per cent of the wage differential. Furthermore, our results suggest that a large part of the

Table 5.6. Decomposition of $\ln(W_f/W_m)$ for married men and women GHS 1975

Equations used in the decomposition	(a) Percentage due to differences in attributes	(b) Percentage due to non-participation	(c) Percentage due to differences in coefficients	Total	(Actual $W_f/W_m = 0.623$) Estimated value of relative wage (W_f/W_m) if discrimination was eliminated	
					Assuming (b) and (c) are due to discrimination	Assuming only (c) is due to discrimination
1. Small specification (Table 5.4)						
(1) — (2)	2.7	–	97.3	100	0.987	0.987
(1) — (3)	11.1	50.1	38.8	100	0.949	0.748
(1) — (4)	11.1	69.7	19.2	100	0.949	0.682
2. Large specification (Table 5.5)						
(1) — (2)	28.1	–	71.9	100	0.876	0.876
(1) — (3)	31.4	40.1	28.5	100	0.862	0.713
(1) — (4)	31.4	57.0	11.6	100	0.862	0.658

Notes: (i) The decomposition used is $\ln(W_m) - \ln(W_f) = \boldsymbol{\alpha}(\mathbf{X}_m - \mathbf{X}_f) - \mathbf{H}_f\boldsymbol{\beta}_h + \mathbf{X}_f(\boldsymbol{\alpha} - \boldsymbol{\beta})$, and is explained in the text.
(ii) The small specifications include only education and experience variables. The large specifications include in addition 10 dummies for occupational groups, 23 dummies for industrial sectors, 1 dummy for race and 1 dummy for health.
(iii) (1) Wage equation for married men. (2) Wage equation for married women with 'potential experience'. (3) Wage equation for married women with 'actual experience' and 'home time'. (4) As equation (3) but corrected for selectivity bias.

remaining differential is due to the effect of non-participation. For each year that a woman does not participate, we have estimated a decrease in earnings capacity of about 3 per cent and we estimate that in our sample married women spend on average about 7 years outside the labour market. In all, this factor explains 50 per cent of the wage differential, being by far the most important of those considered in our specification, and leaving a residual of less than 40 per cent. The measurement of discrimination now depends on whether we take the percentage explained by non-participation as being discriminatory or not. If non-participation does actually lead to a depreciation of productive skills, then the differential in pay explained by this factor should not be interpreted as being discriminatory. However, to the extent that non-participation could simply be used by employers as an excuse for paying women less than they would pay men of equivalent productive characteristics, then this percentage ought to be interpreted as being discriminatory. It is impossible to know which of these two assumptions is more realistic, so in Table 5.6 we measure discrimination under both interpretations. If the wage gap due to non-participation and the wage gap due to differences in the market rewards of given characteristics (columns (b) and (c) of Table 5.6) are both considered to be discriminatory, then the elimination of discrimination would raise the relative wage from 0.623 to 0.949. However, if we only consider discriminatory that latter part, then the elimination of discrimination would raise the relative wage to only 0.748; that is, the wages of married women would still be 25 per cent lower than those of married men.

As the third row of Table 5.6 indicates, correcting for selectivity bias reinforces the conclusions just reached. The part of the wage gap explained by non-participation increases to almost 70 per cent and the residual goes down to 19 per cent.[33] Eliminating discrimination would also raise the relative wage to 0.948 if both (b) and (c) are considered to be discriminatory, but it would only raise it to 0.682 if only (c) were taken to be discriminatory, which is just 9.5 per cent higher than the actual differential.[34]

The results obtained when the large specifications are used (bottom part of Table 5.6) reduce as expected the extent of discrimination (the unexplained residual). By inflating the part explained by differences in endowments, they also reduce the percentage of the gap explained by the non-participation effect, but this still remains the largest of the three effects. Taking account of the occupational and industrial distributions does not alter our previous qualitative results, thus we offer these figures as a lower bound estimate of discrimination effects. A subsidiary result that we obtain from this analysis is a measure of the wage gap due to differences in the distribution of male and female employment across industries and occupations. Using actual experience (i.e. the comparisons $(1) - (3)$ or $(1) - (4)$ in Table 5.6), the difference in the male–female employment structure would explain 20.3 per cent of the wage gap $(31.4 - 11.1)$.

These results suggest that the extent of discrimination between married men and married women is much smaller than what a conventional approach to the problem (i.e. the comparisons $(1) - (2)$ in Table 5.6) would lead one to think. This conclusion may appear somewhat at variance with existing presumptions about the problem, but we would like to point out that, in addition to the similarities of equivalent estimates with US data discussed above, our results on discrimination are very similar to those obtained in the UK for men and single women by Greenhalgh (1980). That is, our results point to the (in our opinion reasonable) conclusion that discrimination against married women is not greater than that against single women. The labour market treats married women with a given level of experience as it would treat single women with that same experience, and the extent of discrimination towards single women is far smaller than that suggested by the comparisons $(1) - (2)$ in Table 5.6.

What do these results tell us about the effectiveness of equal pay legislation? The answer to this question clearly depends on the extent of discrimination that may exist and this, as we have seen above, depends on the assumptions we make as to whether the percentage of the wage gap explained by non-participation is to be considered discriminatory or not. Since there is little we can say about this on the basis of our data, we present here the results that correspond to the two extreme assumptions used above. Since there is also ambiguity as to whether the present male–female distribution of employment across industries and occupations is the result of choice (and its results in terms of pay do not therefore qualify as discriminatory) or the result of imposed segregation (in which case the resulting pay differentials are discriminatory), we will use in our evaluation an average of the results obtained with the small specifications of Table 5.4 (which interpret the structure of employment as being totally the result of imposed segregation) and those obtained with the large specifications of Table 5.5 (which interpret this structure as the result of voluntary choice on the part of women).

Using the comparison $(1)-(3)$ in Table 5.6 and assuming that the percentages (b) and (c) are both discriminatory, the complete elimination of discrimination as seen from 1975 would involve an increase in female relative pay from 0.623 to 0.905 (the average of 0.949 and 0.862). That is, a percentage increase in the female relative wage of 45.3 per cent. As we have seen in Chapter 4 above, by 1975 most of the effects of the equal pay legislation (an increase in female relative pay of 18.8 per cent) had already taken place, so it is reasonable to assume that the figures used in the present analysis already incorporate these gains. We have then that, as compared with the pre-legislation situation (that is, compared with 1970), the total potential increase needed to eliminate discrimination would be 64.1 per cent. Of this total, equal pay legislation has managed to achieve an increase of 18.8 per cent. That is, it has achieved 29.3 per cent of the total potential increase. If, on the other hand, we assume that only the percentage (c) is discriminatory, repeating the analysis we find that out of a total potential increase of 36.1 per cent, the legislation has achieved 18.8 per cent. That is, 52.1 per cent of the total possible gain. The conclusion therefore is that, depending on assumptions made, equal pay legislation would have managed to achieve between 30 and 50 per cent of the total possible gains needed to eliminate discrimination completely.

The whole analysis can be repeated using the comparisons $(1)-(4)$ in Table 5.6. These comparisons are not conditional on the current participation of women in the labour market, while the previous $(1)-(3)$ comparisons are between men who currently work and women who also currently work. Under the assumption that both (b) and (c) are discriminatory, the conclusion from this unconditional comparison would be that the legislation has managed 29.3 per cent of the total possible gains, and under the assumption that only (c) is discriminatory, that it has managed 71.5 per cent of the total possible gains.

5.5 Summary and conclusions

The main concern of this chapter has been the wage differential that exists between married men and married women, as measured with data from the *General Household Survey* of 1975. Together with education, labour market experience is one of the most important determinants of earnings capacity, and has therefore figured prominently in the study of wage structures. The problem with GHS data (and with most other cross-sectional sources) is that for married women at least, there is very poor information on this variable. The nearest variable usually considered is age minus school-leaving age, but this for married women is an acknowledged poor proxy for market experience. Two other problems that the analysis of earnings structures has to face are the endogeneity of accumulated market experience, and the selectivity bias that results from the truncated sample on which wage equations have to be estimated.

In this chapter we have proposed a method of analysis that deals with these three problems by interpreting the wage equation as part of a larger labour supply model. This allows us to predict accumulated labour market experience in terms of exogenous variables concerning characteristics of married women and their families, to apportion the total period of time since leaving school between actual experience and time spent at home. We found that our prediction procedure yields estimates of actual experience and home time which are very close to those obtained by Stewart and Greenhalgh (1982) from retrospective data in the *National Training Survey*. This provides a strong test of our model and suggests that cross-sectional data can be helpful in order to infer past working histories.

Our results suggest that the problems of measurement, endogeneity and selectivity are empirically important. When market experience is measured properly and when its endogenous nature is taken into account, the percentage of the wage gap explained by differences in attributes increases substantially. Married women are at a disadvantage in terms of wage rates for two main reasons. First, because they possess less accumulated market experience (and presumably have accumulated less post-school training), and second, because that part of the potential working life they spend at home severely depresses their earning capacity (possibly due to depreciation of their market skills).

The measurement of discrimination depends on whether we assume that the depressant effect of non-participation on wages is discriminatory or not. If we assume that it is, we have estimated that as compared with the pre-legislation situation, the total increase in female relative pay needed to eliminate discrimination would have been 64 per cent. Of this total, the legislation has managed to achieve about 19 per cent, which represents almost 30 per cent of the total potential increase. If we assume that the depressant effect of non-participation is only reflecting depreciation in market skills and is therefore non-discriminatory, then the total potential gain would have been 36 per cent. So in this case, the 19 per cent increase achieved by the legislation would represent more than 52 per cent of the total potential increase.

Perhaps the most interesting result of this chapter is the relationship we have uncovered between female low pay and female non-participation in the labour market. Our data are not the most suitable to actually find out how this relationship arises and to what extent the resulting pay differential can be considered discriminatory or not. But we think our results are sufficiently robust to suggest that more effort should be devoted to the investigation of these matters. We have had to use indirect methods to infer the amount of years of non-participation, and we have only been able to derive accumulated figures of market experience and home time. Much better and more reliable results could probably be obtained with longitudinal data, giving information not only on the actual amount of market and home periods, but also on the timing of these changes in status and on the progression of female workers through the occupational and industrial structure as they go in and out of the labour force.

Annex to chapter 1

The Equal Pay Act and the Sex Discrimination Act

Here we present extracts from the *Guide to the Equal Pay Act*, relating to the provisions of the Equal Pay and Sex Discrimination Acts, published by the Department of Employment (Revised Edition, January 1976). Numbers refer to paragraphs of the above mentioned *Guide*. We also make some comments on the amendment of the Equal Pay Act introduced in 1983 and prompted by the accession of Britain to the European Community.

The Equal Pay Act

Introduction

1. The Equal Pay Act 1970 came into force on 29 December 1975. Its purpose is to eliminate discrimination between men and women in regard to pay and other terms of their contracts of employment (e.g. overtime, bonus, output and piecework payments, holiday and sick-leave entitlement). It seeks to achieve this purpose in two main ways:

(i) by establishing the right of the individual woman to equal treatment in respect of terms of her contract of employment when she is employed:

(a) on work of the same or a broadly similar nature to that of a man;

(b) in a job which, though different from that of a man, has been given an equal value to the man's job under evaluation;

and

(ii) by providing for the Central Arbitration Committee to remove discrimination in collective agreements, employers' pay structures and statutory wage orders which contain any provisions applying specifically to men only or to women only and which have been referred to the Committee.

2. . . .

3. The Act applies both to men and to women . . . References . . . to the right of a woman to equal treatment with a man are to be understood as including also the right of a man to equal treatment with a woman. The Act does not, however, confer any rights on people to claim equal treatment with other people of the same sex.

Rights of individual women to equal treatment

4.   An individual woman has a right to equal treatment with a man when she is employed on like work to that of a man . . . or employed in a job which, even if different from that of a man, has been given an equal value to the man's job under evaluation . . . unless the employer can show that any variation in their treatment is genuinely due to a material difference (other than the difference of sex) between her case and his . . .

5.   Equal treatment does not necessarily mean identical treatment. It means either:

(a) that each term in a woman's contract of employment must be not less favourable than the corresponding term in the man's contract; or

(b) that where the man has a term in his contract, . . . the woman is entitled to the same treatment as the man in that respect, . . .

Area of comparison

6.   The comparisons which a woman may draw with a man or with a man's job are limited to men employed by her employer or an associated employer. Two employers are associated if one is a company of which the other (directly or indirectly) has control . . .

7.   Such comparisons are normally limited to men employed at the same establishment. However, comparisons may be drawn with men at another establishment if both establishments are owned by the same employer (or an associated employer) and if terms and conditions of employment are common to the two establishments . . .

8.   . . .

Like work

9.   A woman is regarded as employed on like work to that of a man where she is doing the same work as he is or work of a broadly similar nature provided that the differences, if any, between the things she does and the things he does are not of practical importance in relation to terms and conditions of employment . . .

Job evaluation

10.   Where:

(i) job evaluation has been carried out; and

(ii) a job carried out by a woman has been given an equal value with a job carried out by a man; and

(iii) any terms of the contracts of employment of employees are based on the job evaluation;

then the man and the woman concerned must be treated equally in relation to any such terms . . .

11.   Job evaluation is defined as being a study undertaken with a view to evaluating, in terms of the demand made on a worker under various

headings (for instance, effort, skill, decision), the jobs to be done by all or any of the employees in an undertaking or group of undertakings . . . There is no requirement in the Act to undertake job evaluation . . .
12.   In general, the Act takes the results of job evaluation as they stand and is directed to requiring the equalization of the terms of the contracts of employment which are based on the evaluation . . .

Material differences
13.   Where it has been established, or agreed, that a woman is doing the same or broadly similar work to that of a man or work that has been rated as equivalent under a job evaluation, she is entitled to equal treatment unless the employer can show that any variation between the woman's contract and the man's contract is *'genuinely* due to a material difference (other than the difference of sex)' between her case and his . . .

Application to an industrial tribunal
14.   A woman who believes that she has a right to equal treatment with a man, because she is engaged in the same or broadly similar work, or on work which has been rated as equivalent under job evaluation, but whose employer does not agree with her, may apply to an industrial tribunal for a decision . . .
15.   . . .
16.   . . .
17.   A woman may make an application to an industrial tribunal at any time while she is doing the job to which the claim relates, or within six months after date of termination of that job . . .
18.   A woman may claim arrears of remuneration in respect of a period of up to two years before the date on which she makes an application to a tribunal. She may claim damages in respect of non-cash benefits up to the same limit of two years. There is, however, no claim to arrears of remuneration or damages in respect of a period before 29 December 1975 . . .
19.   Where there is disagreement, an employer may apply to a tribunal for an order declaring the rights of the employer and the employee in relation to the matter in question . . .
20.   . . .

Advice and assistance
21.   At a tribunal hearing, both the person making the complaint and the person against whom it is made can be represented by anyone they choose, e.g. a solicitor, or a representative of a trade union, or an employers' association, or anyone else.
22.   . . .
23.   . . .
24.   The Equal Opportunities Commission . . . has the power to assist individuals in presenting complaints and conducting legal proceedings

where the complaint raises a question of principle or where there are other special considerations.

25.   The Secretary of State may make a reference to an industrial tribunal where it appears to him that a woman has a claim to equal treatment but that it is not reasonable to expect her to take steps to make the reference herself . . .

Conciliation
26.   . . .

Appeals
27.   . . .

Collective agreements
28.   A collective agreement which contains any provision 'applying specifically to men only or to women only' may be referred to the Central Arbitration Committee for amendment with a view to removing the discrimination between men and women . . .
29.   The Committee must first amend the agreement to extend to both men and women any provision applying specifically to men only, or to women only . . . The Committee must eliminate the duplication (of different wage rates between men and women) by striking out the lower rate. The final result would, therefore, be a single rate of pay for the category of work (or workers) in question, applicable to all the workers concerned irrespective of sex, and equal in amount to the former men's rate of pay . . .
30.   . . .
31.   An agreement may lay down a rate of pay for women workers only in a particular category while making no provision for men in the same category because, for example, there are at the time, no men doing that kind of work. In such a case if a rate of pay applying to women only is lower than the lowest rate of pay applying to men in the agreement, the Committee is required to raise the rate applying to women to the level of the lowest rate applicable to men . . .
32.   . . .
33.   . . .
34.   The Committee is required to make similar amendments to those described in paragraphs 28–33 to collective agreements referred to it which discriminate between men and women in respect of terms of employment other than rates of pay . . .
35.   The Central Arbitration Committee may specify a date before or after its decision on which its amendments shall become effective, provided that the date is not before the date of reference. Different dates may be specified for different amendments . . .

Employers' pay structures

36.   The provisions of the Act relating to collective agreements apply also to employers' pay structures . . .

Wage orders

37.   Orders made by a wages council, a statutory joint industrial council or by an agricultural wages board may also be referred to the Central Arbitration Committee for a declaration of the amendments which may need to be made to an order to remove discrimination between men and women . . .

38.   . . .

39.   . . .

References to the Committee

40.   . . .

People covered by the Act

41.   The rights of individual workers to equal treatment (paragraphs 4 to 27) extend to all people employed under a contract of service or of apprenticeship, or a contract personally to execute any work or labour . . . No people are excepted from the provisions of the Act because they work part-time, or in small firms, or because they have been in their present job for only a short time. People employed wholly or mainly outside Great Britain are, however, excepted from these provisions . . .

42.   . . .

43.   . . .

44.   . . .

45.   . . .

46.   The Act does not extend to Northern Ireland, which is covered by separate legislation . . .

Terms of employment covered by the Act

47.   The Act extends to all matters covered by an employee's contract of employment and all provisions of a collective agreement, pay structure or wages order . . .

48.   The Act does not allow discrimination in relation to terms related to marriage . . .

49.   Certain matters are excepted from the general requirement of the Act that there should be no discrimination between men and women in regard to the terms of a woman's employment. Thus, where the terms of a woman's employment are affected by compliance with the laws regulating the employment of women – e.g. Part VI of the Factories Act – the Act does not require men and women to be treated equally . . .

50.   The Act does not require men and women to be treated equally to the extent that women may be given special treatment in connection with the birth or expected birth of a child . . .

51.   Nor is equal treatment required as regards terms 'related to death or retirement'. Retirement includes retirement, 'whether voluntary or not, on grounds of age, length of service, or incapacity' . . .

52.   There is, however, an exception to this exclusion. Since 6 April 1978 . . . , where a man has membership of an occupational pension scheme as a term of his contract of employment, a woman with a right to equal treatment with him must also be given, as a term of her contract, access to membership of the scheme on terms which are the same as to the age and length of service needed for becoming a member and as to whether membership is voluntary or obligatory . . .

Armed Forces and the Police

53.   The general provisions of the Act do not apply to the Armed Forces and the Police.

54.   The Armed Forces (men's and women's services) are covered by a special provision . . .

55.   . . .

The Equal Opportunities Commission

56.   A public body, the Equal Opportunities Commission, was set up under the Sex Discrimination Act. It has the following duties:

    (a) to work towards the elimination of discrimination;

    (b) to promote equality of opportunity between men and women generally;

and

    (c) to keep under review the working of the Sex Discrimination Act and the Equal Pay Act . . .

    . . .

The Sex Discrimination Act

57.   The Sex Discrimination Act makes it unlawful for an employer to treat a woman, on the ground of sex, less favourably than he treats or would treat a man, in respect to access to jobs and all non-contractual benefits of employment (other than benefits relating to retirement and death). The Sex Discrimination Act also applies to benefits covered by contracts of employment, other than benefits consisting of the payment of money, in situations where a woman is not employed on like work or work rated as equivalent to that of a man . . .

58.   The Sex Discrimination Act also makes it unlawful for an employer to treat a married person, on the ground of being married, less favourably than a single person of the same sex is, or would be, treated. In addition, it makes unlawful indirect discrimination, defined as the application of a requirement or condition with which considerably fewer women than men (or considerably fewer married than single people) can comply, and which cannot be shown to be justifiable.

59. It is also unlawful, under the Sex Discrimination Act, to discriminate against any person by treating her less favourably than another person on the grounds that the person victimized has asserted her rights under the Equal Pay Act or Sex Discrimination Act or has been associated with any action taken with reference to either Act.

60. Complaints of discrimination in the employment field under the Sex Discrimination Act, like cases under the Equal Pay Act, are dealt with by industrial tribunals.

61. ...

The Equal Pay (Amendment) Regulations 1983

As from 1 January 1984, changes were introduced to the Equal Pay Act 1970 (upon which our analysis in this book has been based) to give effect to the 'equal pay for work of equal value' principle. Though our conclusions for the effects of the original Act remain unaltered, we present below the basic amendments with some considerations as to the possible effects of the new legislation.

The amendment of the Equal Pay Act, 1970 was prompted by:

(a) The accession of Britain to the European Community (EEC) on 1 January 1973 and her subsequent obligation to comply with Community laws as other member states. The Treaty of Rome (1958), Article 119, set forth the principle that 'men and women should receive equal pay for equal work' which was further clarified by the Council Directive 75/117/EEC (The Equal Pay Directive) of 10 February 1975.

(b) The EEC's infringement procedures against Britain for failure to implement Article 1 of the Equal Pay Directive (op. cit.) which declares that 'the principle of equal pay' in article 119 of the Treaty of Rome 'means, for the same work or *for work to which equal value is attributed*, the elimination of *all* discrimination on grounds of sex with respect to *all* aspects and conditions or remuneration' (emphasis added to show where the Equal Pay Act 1970 fell short of the Directive). The European Court of Justice in Luxembourg gave judgement on 6 July 1982 to the effect that Britain had failed to fulfil her obligations under the Treaty of Rome.

As a result, the 'equality clause' of the Equal Pay Act, 1970 (para. 1, p. 97), which deemed that the right to equal treatment applied to a woman employed on 'like work' (sub-para. i(a), op. cit.) or work which had been rated 'equivalent' under a job evaluation study (sub-para. i(b), op. cit), was extended in the Equal Pay (Amendment) Regulations, 1983, to include a third sub-paragraph for a woman who is employed on work which is 'in terms of the demands made on her (for instance, under such headings as effort, skill and decision) of equal value to that of a man in the same establishment'.

Also, under the Amendment, the procedure of making an 'equal value' claim starts in the same way as other equal pay claims, i.e. with the sub-mission of a claim by an employee to an Industrial Tribunal (paras. 14–17, p. 99). If the claim is not withdrawn or settled, the Tribunal has first to decide whether it falls under the 'like' or 'equivalent' provisions, and if it does, the original Act applies. However, if the claim does not come under these two headings, the Tribunal will then have to decide whether there are grounds for determining that the jobs are of 'equal value'. If there are no such grounds, the claim will be dismissed at this stage. If there are grounds for determining that the jobs in question are of equal value, the Tribunal may hear the employer's defence at this stage and either dismiss the case or commission a report from independent experts which, together with the evidence produced by the interested parties, will form the basis upon which the Tribunal will award equal pay or dismiss the claim. It is at the discretion of the Tribunal to hear the employer's defence first, or to go straight for the experts' report.

Thus, the Equal Pay (Amendment) Regulations, 1983, made some progress in meeting the criticisms of the European Court. However, the new text takes the form of an extremely complex series of technical amendments to the existing Equal Pay Act, 1970, and still falls short of Community requirements. In particular:

(a) The woman still has to compare herself with a man in '*the same establishment*', unlike, say, the Dutch Equal Pay Act, 1975, where, in the absence of comparable work in an establishment, comparison can be made to a 'man's job in a similar establishment in the same trade or industry'.

(b) The woman's work is compared to contemporaneous male work in the same establishment, and it is not possible for her to claim what a man would get if he *were* doing her job.

(c) 'Equal value' claims are subject to a *different* and *harder* procedure than the 'like' or 'equivalent' work claims (see above).

(d) Tribunals now have new powers to consider employers' arguments *before* the substance of the case has been examined and to dismiss an application at this early stage if such arguments are accepted.

(e) The Amendment Regulations contain no procedure for dealing with collective agreements which prevent equal pay for work of 'equal value'.

(f) The complexity of the new text is 'beyond compare . . . (and) no ordinary lawyer will be able to understand . . . and the industrial tribunals would have the greatest difficulty and the Court of Appeal would probably be divided in opinion' (Lord Denning, H.L. Deb., Vol. 445, cols. 901–2, 5 December 1983).

Our findings suggest that the effects of the original Act came mostly through the abolition of discriminatory wage rates in Collective Agreements (para. 1, ii, p. 97 and paras. 28–35, p. 100). This view is now shared in subsequent research (see, for example, Snell *et al.* (1981), or Hepple

(1984)). Will the sharp and once-for-all gains in female pay during the early 1970s be reinforced by the new Act? Our view is that they will, and there has already been a successful claim under the 'equal value' clause: an Industrial Tribunal upheld a claim by a qualified woman cook to be paid the same wage as a male joiner, a painter and a thermal insulations engineer also employed in the same company (Julie Hayward v. Cammel Laird Shipbuilders, 1984). The woman's pay was increased by a staggering 30 per cent (from £99 to £130 a week), i.e. to the level given to skilled outfitters. This of course is an isolated case from which it is not possible to make a generalization, but it illustrates new ways in which the 'equal value' principle can be applied. A final evaluation of the effects of this amendment, however, will have to wait some time and to consider also the influence that these likely increases in pay could have on female employment.

Annex to chapter 2

Data used in the decomposition analysis

Table A2.1. *Relative employment and wages of full-time and part-time women 1972–79 (per cent)*

Year	Manual workers		Non-manual workers		All workers	
	F/M	W_f/W_m	F/M	W_f/W_m	F/M	W_f/W_m
1972	32.28	58.96	85.74	51.82	51.93	59.51
1973	31.40	59.90	84.48	52.28	51.39	59.82
1974	31.65	62.36	85.01	52.91	51.83	61.07
1975	28.70	66.36	83.52	58.23	50.70	66.15
1976	30.29	68.67	86.92	59.77	53.28	68.10
1977	31.46	69.05	88.13	61.22	54.75	68.51
1978	31.70	68.95	88.15	58.62	55.23	66.96
1979	31.94	66.98	90.50	58.38	56.39	66.04

Notes: See notes to Table 2.1.
Source: New Earnings Survey, 1970 to 1980.

Table A2.2. *Relative (F/M) hourly earnings excluding overtime effects of full-time manual employees (per cent)*

	Industry group	70	71	72	73	74	75	76	77	78	79	80
I	Agriculture, forestry, etc.	62.4										
II	Mining and quarrying											
III	Food, drink and tobacco	62.4	63.3	65.2	66.7	69.1	72.8	75.7	77.8	76.8	74.3	74.5
IV	Coal and petroleum products											
V	Chemicals and allied industries	59.1	57.4	58.1	59.9	61.7	64.6	69.5	69.8	69.1	68.7	68.4
VI	Metal manufacture										69.3	67.8
VII	Mechanical engineering	62.8	63.3	65.4	65.6	68.1	72.1	75.3	76.7	76.3	75.9	75.0
VIII	Instrument engineering	61.8	64.8	64.1	65.2	65.9		76.8		75.7	75.4	74.1
IX	Electrical engineering	64.6	62.4	64.3	64.7	67.7	71.1	75.7	75.3	74.4	74.5	72.9
X	Shipbuilding and marine engineering											
XI	Vehicles	63.4	60.1	62.1	63.0	68.3	60.6	78.0	77.8	79.3	77.1	77.4
XII	Metal goods not elsewhere specified	61.3	59.7	60.0	60.1	62.2		74.0	73.9	73.7	71.8	72.0
XIII	Textiles	61.3	63.9	64.6	65.8	66.7	70.5	71.6	73.0	75.2	73.1	73.1
XIV	Leather, leather goods and fur											
XV	Clothing and footwear	62.7	63.7	63.0	63.5	65.7	71.5	71.8	73.7	72.7	71.6	73.3
XVI	Bricks, pottery, glass, cement, etc.	66.4	65.1	67.2	62.5	65.7	70.1	73.3	75.5	75.1	71.7	71.1
XVII	Timber, furniture, etc.										79.1	
XVIII	Paper, printing and publishing	54.0	52.9	53.7	56.3	58.0	64.9	69.1	68.7	69.4	66.1	66.9
XIX	Other manufacturing industries	59.8	57.8	58.2	60.0	61.5	64.0	67.4	67.4	68.4	66.6	69.5
XX	Construction											
XXI	Gas, electricity and water											
XXII	Transport and communication	79.1	74.6	75.0	74.3	75.5	80.7	80.7	79.9	83.0	79.2	81.6
XXIII	Distributive trades	62.8	62.3	63.2	64.2	66.2	69.7	73.9	74.9	75.2	73.5	75.8
XXIV	Insurance, banking, finance and business services											
XXV	Professional and scientific services	65.6	68.7	72.3	73.4	80.0	81.7	83.5	83.3	83.7	80.5	79.0
XXVI	Miscellaneous services	59.3	61.6	62.5	64.5	64.8	70.8	75.5	74.9	74.2	73.3	74.7
XXVII	Public administration and defence	71.4	76.1	80.1	81.0	80.9	82.2	84.3	86.8	84.8	82.5	81.2
	All industries	61.7	61.3	61.8	62.0	64.4	68.0	71.1	71.7	72.0	70.2	70.9

Source: *New Earnings Survey*, 1970 to 1980.

Table A2.3. Relative (F/M) hourly earnings excluding overtime effects of full-time non-manual employees (per cent)

	Industry group	70	71	72	73	74	75	76	77	78	79	80
I	Agriculture, forestry, etc.											
II	Mining and quarrying											
III	Food, drink and tobacco				48.5		56.4	57.4	59.3	57.4	59.8	57.6
IV	Coal and petroleum products											
V	Chemicals and allied industries	42.9	46.0	46.6	45.3	49.6	51.4	51.9	53.9	59.2	53.6	52.0
VI	Metal manufacture		48.6	46.6	50.6		58.3	60.2	59.0	59.2	61.2	56.6
VII	Mechanical engineering		47.3	47.1	48.0	48.9	55.8	55.9	56.9	55.6	55.8	56.5
VIII	Instrument engineering										53.1	54.8
IX	Electrical engineering	44.0	46.8	47.5	47.0	50.2	54.2	58.0	58.6	56.6	58.3	57.4
X	Shipbuilding and marine engineering											
XI	Vehicles	47.5	48.6	49.6	50.7	52.6	58.6	62.0	63.7	61.8	59.0	58.7
XII	Metal goods not elsewhere specified				47.3	50.3	55.5		58.9	56.0	56.6	54.1
XIII	Textiles										50.8	50.2
XIV	Leather, leather goods and fur											
XV	Clothing and footwear											
XVI	Bricks, pottery, glass, cement, etc.										57.8	58.1
XVII	Timber, furniture, etc.										57.0	55.9
XVIII	Paper, printing and publishing			50.9	50.7	52.3		60.9	64.0	62.4	61.3	63.3
XIX	Other manufacturing industries										54.7	57.4
XX	Construction		46.1	46.2	46.5	46.8	51.5	53.0	54.0	54.2	54.4	54.9
XXI	Gas, electricity and water		51.7	51.1	54.3	54.3	57.1	55.6	58.7	57.5	59.6	55.7
XXII	Transport and communication	59.1	58.6	60.3	60.0	61.2	63.3	65.1	66.7	65.7	64.1	65.1
XXIII	Distributive trades	45.6	46.5	46.2	47.6	50.2	54.1	54.4	55.2	54.5	54.1	56.1
XXIV	Insurance, banking, finance and business services	43.2	45.5	45.7	45.9	48.7	51.4	51.0	51.4	51.9	52.5	51.3
XXV	Professional and scientific services	57.1	57.4	59.7	60.4	59.4	67.2	68.4	67.7	64.9	66.0	66.3
XXVI	Miscellaneous services	53.6	56.2	55.5	57.2	61.3		66.7	69.5	67.0	67.3	68.6
XXVII	Public administration and defence	61.3	60.5	62.6	60.5	63.5	62.8	63.4	65.9	65.4	65.1	64.9
	All industries	52.5	53.2	54.0	54.3	55.5	60.7	62.6	63.1	61.2	61.0	61.1

Source: New Earnings Survey, 1970 to 1980.

Table A2.4. *Relative (F/M) hourly earnings excluding overtime effects by occupation, 1973–80 (per cent)*

Occupation group	1973	1974	1975	1976	1977	1978	1979	1980
Non-manual								
Clerical and related	70.7	72.6	74.8	75.4	77.7	78.9	79.3	79.5
Selling	46.0	49.1	52.2	52.0	53.7	52.6	52.5	56.0
Security and protective services					87.5	87.2	85.4	83.7
All non-manual	54.3	55.5	60.7	62.6	63.1	61.2	61.0	61.1
Manual								
Catering, cleaning, etc. and other personal service	72.5	76.0	81.2	83.7	83.9	83.3	82.9	82.5
Processing (excl. metal)	63.1	58.7	66.5	69.2	70.4	71.1	69.4	68.5
Making and repairing (excl. metal)	58.5	60.8	64.2	66.8	67.8	68.5	66.9	67.9
Processing, making etc. (metal and electrical)	61.5	63.5	67.1	71.2	73.3	74.0	73.0	70.4
Painting, assembling, inspecting, packaging etc.	61.2	64.2	68.0	71.6	72.7	72.6	72.0	72.2
Transport, materials, storing and moving	70.5	71.8	75.8	77.4	77.4	77.6	75.9	80.5
All manual	62.0	64.4	68.0	71.1	71.7	72.0	70.2	70.9
All workers	64.4	65.9	70.6	73.5	73.8	72.3	71.3	71.8

Source: New Earnings Survey, 1973 to 1980.

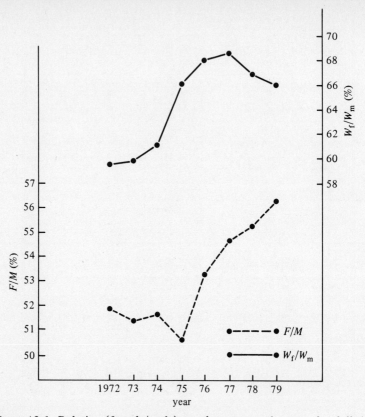

Chart A2.1 Relative (female/male) employment and wages for full-time and part-time workers (manual and non-manual)

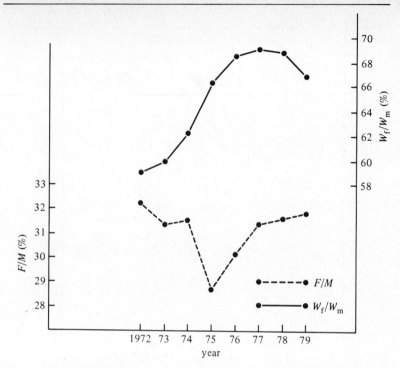

Chart A2.2 Relative (female/male) employment and wages for full-time and part-time manual workers

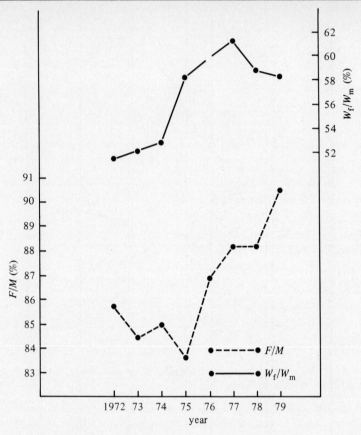

Chart A2.3 Relative (female/male) employment and wages for full-time and part-time non-manual workers

Annex to chapter 3

Changes in collective agreements

The coverage of agreements and the scope of wages boards and councils changed somewhat between 1972 and 1980. We, therefore, present the following information regarding the coverage of the agreements in Table 3.3.

1. Engineering (M): This refers to manual workers in the 'Engineering-manual workers' agreement. The 1972 and 1980 figures cover broadly the same workers. However, the sample size in 1980 was considerably smaller than in 1972 either suggesting changes in the composition of this group or reflecting the fact that less workers were covered by this agreement because of the recession in manufacturing.

2. Engineering (N): This refers to agreement 'Engineering-clerical workers' and, although there is a significant drop in the sample size in 1980, this category broadly covers the same type of workers in both time periods. For this particular group, instead of using 1980 as the final year of comparison we used the year 1979, since there was no information published for this agreement in 1980.

3. Retail co-op: This stands for the 'Retail Co-operative Societies (GB)' agreement and covers both manual and non-manual workers. No change in coverage.

4. and 5. Wages Boards (M) and (N): This refers to manual and non-manual employees respectively covered by wages boards and councils. The coverage differs by the following groups which were excluded in 1980: industrial and staff canteens; boot and floor polish; brush and broom; hair, bass and fibre; hollow-ware; keg and drum; paper box; stamped or pressed metal wares; road haulage. Despite these exclusions, there were still 36 common groups in 1972 and 1980.

6. Local authorities (M): This relates to manual workers NJC in England and Wales and refers to the same groups in 1972 and 1980.

7. Civil servants − clerical: Although the civil servants agreements as covered in the New Earnings Survey were changed in 1975/6, 'Civil

Service–clerical grades' in 1972 has a similar coverage to 'Civil Service Administration group: clerical grades' in 1980, and these are the two agreements in Table 3.3.

8. Government industrial establishments: This refers to manual workers and there was no change in coverage.

9. Ancillary, NHS: This refers to both manual and non-manual employees covered by the agreement 'Ancillary Staff Whitley Council'. In 1980 the ambulancemen were excluded, so the coverage of this agreement has changed somewhat.

10. Teachers: There were not appreciable changes in the coverage of this agreement, and the figures refer to primary and secondary teachers in England and Wales.

Annex to chapter 4

Data and sources of the time-series analysis

Table A4.1 presents the variables used in the estimation of the demand relationship. This Annex details the definition and sources of these variables. The abbreviations used are:

DEG   *Department of Employment Gazette*
NES   *New Earnings Survey*
HA   *Historical Abstract*, Department of Employment
YB   *Yearbook*, Department of Employment
NIE   *National Income and Expenditure*, Central Statistical Office
AAS   *Annual Abstract of Statistics*, Central Statistical Office
FES   *Family Expenditure Survey*

FH/MH: Relative (female/male) employment. This is the ratio of female over male 'total employees in employment' multiplied by the ratio of female over male weekly hours worked. The employment ratio is that at mid-June of each year as given by DEG. After 1959 DEG provides a new series which was linked to the old one using 1959 as the common year. The hours ratio is estimated as follows. For the period 1950 to 1970 female weekly hours (H_f) are obtained as

$$H_f = (PT)(20) + (FT)(WHFM)$$

where PT is the proportion of women in employment working part-time, FT the proportion working full-time, and $WHFM$ is the number of weekly hours of female full-time manual workers, obtained from the AAS. The proportions of part-time and full-time were obtained by linear interpolation from the *Census* of 1951, 1961 and, since 1963, from the FES. For the period 1970 to 1980 H_f is obtained from the NES. Then the two series are linked using 1970 as the common year. Male weekly hours are obtained from the AAS for the period 1950–70 (weekly hours of male manual workers) and from the NES for the period 1970–80. Again, the two are linked using 1970 as the common year.

W_f/W_m: Relative (female/male) hourly earnings. For the period 1950–70 male and female hourly earnings are obtained as follows:

Table A4.1. Variables used in the estimation of the demand equation

Year	FH/MH	(FH/MH)*	W_f/W_m	I	I*	Q/Q*
1950	0.4438	0.4916	0.5959	0.2990	0.3533	1.0413
1951	0.4463	0.4928	0.6028	0.3006	0.3529	1.0240
1952	0.4346	0.4788	0.6014	0.2976	0.3481	0.9853
1953	0.4393	0.4846	0.5987	0.2996	0.3501	0.9928
1954	0.4386	0.4823	0.5945	0.3008	0.3494	1.0014
1955	0.4339	0.4737	0.5888	0.2982	0.3450	1.0048
1956	0.4300	0.4664	0.5870	0.2991	0.3441	0.9865
1957	0.4248	0.4557	0.6004	0.3033	0.3469	0.9751
1958	0.4196	0.4490	0.5883	0.3034	0.3470	0.9470
1959	0.4170	0.4420	0.5953	0.3062	0.3484	0.9642
1960	0.4156	0.4354	0.5957	0.3069	0.3460	0.9887
1961	0.4118	0.4274	0.6033	0.3088	0.3453	0.9825
1962	0.4148	0.4282	0.5949	0.3125	0.3477	0.9714
1963	0.4135	0.4240	0.5952	0.3155	0.3489	0.9786
1964	0.4144	0.4207	0.5857	0.3168	0.3474	1.0142
1965	0.4212	0.4236	0.5884	0.3186	0.3461	1.0178
1966	0.4278	0.4248	0.5865	0.3211	0.3457	1.0128
1967	0.4298	0.4219	0.5890	0.3228	0.3442	1.0080
1968	0.4315	0.4236	0.5764	0.3267	0.3454	1.0285
1969	0.4371	0.4242	0.5802	0.3286	0.3445	1.0270
1970	0.4448	0.4260	0.5797	0.3305	0.3436	1.0233
1971	0.4539	0.4246	0.5882	0.3347	0.3409	1.0166
1972	0.4596	0.4326	0.5951	0.3415	0.3468	1.0280
1973	0.4704	0.4367	0.5982	0.3408	0.3432	1.0677
1974	0.4876	0.4613	0.6107	0.3340	0.3427	1.0282
1975	0.5087	0.4672	0.6615	0.3429	0.3403	0.9902
1976	0.5070	0.4476	0.6810	0.3558	0.3520	0.9886
1977	0.5086	0.4472	0.6851	0.3550	0.3508	0.9852
1978	0.5111	0.4516	0.6696	0.3596	0.3568	0.9893
1979	0.5171	0.4579	0.6604	0.3594	0.3583	0.9850
1980	0.5231	0.4587	0.6657	0.3643	0.3616	0.9411

Note: (FH/MH)* and I* refer to the corresponding variables in the private sector.
Source: See text.

Table A4.2. Instrumental variables used in the 2SLS estimation of the demand equation

Year	FI	Y	U
1950	0.4093	100.0	1.5
1951	0.3980	102.0	1.1
1952	0.3798	105.6	1.6
1953	0.3734	114.5	1.5
1954	0.3706	116.7	1.3
1955	0.3707	115.5	1.0
1956	0.3765	109.0	1.0
1957	0.3850	120.6	1.3
1958	0.3939	123.6	1.9
1959	0.4039	135.0	2.0
1960	0.4175	133.4	1.5
1961	0.4293	135.2	1.3
1962	0.4397	132.1	1.8
1963	0.4483	141.5	2.2
1964	0.4579	149.2	1.6
1965	0.4628	148.8	1.3
1966	0.4639	148.7	1.4
1967	0.4620	157.3	2.2
1968	0.4586	163.3	2.3
1969	0.4510	159.6	2.3
1970	0.4430	156.3	2.5
1971	0.4361	175.7	3.3
1972	0.4239	179.2	3.6
1973	0.4074	192.5	2.6
1974	0.3890	173.0	2.5
1975	0.3681	174.7	3.9
1976	0.3450	188.4	5.2
1977	0.3264	195.6	5.6
1978	0.3152	208.5	5.6
1979	0.3117	195.4	5.2
1980	0.3139	193.3	6.7

Source: See text.

Table A4.3. Correlation matrix of the variables used in the regressions

	FH/MH	(FH/MH)*	W_f/W_m	I	Q/Q*	T	D71	D72	D74	D75	IP	FI	Y	U
FH/MH	1.00	0.29	0.86	0.83	−0.03	0.73	0.89	0.90	0.91	0.86	0.54	−0.75	0.73	0.87
(FH/MH)*		1.00	0.26	−0.29	−0.10	−0.42	0.03	0.11	0.21	0.17	−0.03	−0.64	−0.41	−0.12
W_f/W_m			1.00	0.71	−0.37	0.61	0.73	0.80	0.92	0.96	0.60	−0.81	0.61	0.81
I				1.00	0.03	0.98	0.86	0.84	0.77	0.77	0.54	−0.38	0.97	0.95
Q/Q*					1.00	0.02	0.05	0.01	−0.26	−0.36	0.11	0.43	0.08	−0.19
T						1.00	0.81	0.79	0.72	0.68	0.47	−0.26	0.98	0.89
D71							1.00	0.93	0.78	0.71	0.56	−0.56	0.83	0.86
D72								1.00	0.84	0.77	0.60	−0.63	0.80	0.84
D74									1.00	0.91	0.48	−0.73	0.69	0.82
D75										1.00	0.54	−0.75	0.67	0.85
IP											1.00	−0.44	0.57	0.55
FI												1.00	−0.28	−0.55
Y													1.00	0.89
U														1.00

$$W_f = \alpha(W_f^m) + (1 - \alpha)(W_f^{nm})$$

where α is the proportion of female workers in manual employment, including saleswomen, and is obtained from the Censuses, W_f^m is hourly earnings of female manual workers obtained from the April series of DEG, and W_f^{nm} is hourly earnings of female non-manual workers obtained using the October series of the DEG. The October series are adjusted to express them as of April. For men

$$W_m = \beta(W_m^m) + (1 - \beta)(W_m^{nm})$$

where β is the proportion of male manual workers obtained from the Censuses, W_m^m is the hourly earnings of male manual workers obtained in a similar way as for women, and so on. For the period 1970–80 the corresponding data are obtained from the NES, which includes both full and part-time employees. Before 1970, only data on full-time employees are available. The two series are linked using 1970 as the common year, and adjusting the pre-1970 data to the NES data. So the variable refers to all employees (full and part-time).

Q/Q^*: Relative deviations from trend of GDP. Q is the actual real GDP index and Q^* is its trend value obtained by regression. The GDP index is obtained from NIE.

I: Industrial index. The index is based on 22 sectors, which cover approximately 99 per cent of total employment (they correspond to 25 sectors in the industrial classification used after 1968; *Standard Industrial Classification*, 1968). The proportions of male and female employment in each sector were obtained from the NES for the period 1968 to 1980, and from the HA before 1968. The common year 1968 was used to link the two series.

Table A4.2 gives the variables used as instruments in the 2SLS estimation of the demand relationship.

FI: Fertility index. This is the number of live births in the last five years per thousand women aged 15 to 44 in the United Kingdom (AAS).

Y: Non-labour real income (1950 = 100). This is defined as GDP minus income from employment, deflated by the Retail Price Index (NIE).

U: Rate of male unemployment. This excludes school leavers and is given as an annual average (DEG).

Finally, Table A4.3 gives the correlation matrices for these variables.

Annex to chapter 5

Data and additional regressions

Table A5.1 gives the indices for real female manual hourly earnings and real male manual weekly earnings used to adjust predicted wages and family income for the increase in real earnings. From 1931 to 1938 they are obtained from the index of real wage earnings given in A.H. Halsey (ed.) *Trends in British Society since 1900* (Table 4.10). From 1938 to 1970 they are obtained from *British Labour Statistics, Historical Abstract 1886–1968*, Department of Employment (Tables 40 to 42 and 46 to 48). To link the two series we used 1938 as the common year. Finally, from 1970 onwards the data are taken from the *New Earnings Survey*, and 1970 is the common year used to link this with the previous series.

Estimated female wages and family income for year t, $\hat{w}_t$ and $\hat{y}_t$ respectively, were then adjusted as follows

$$w_t^* = \hat{w}_t \frac{\text{Index of female manual hourly earnings (year } t)}{\text{Index of female manual hourly earnings (year 1975)}}$$

$$y_t^* = \hat{y}_t \frac{\text{Index of male manual weekly earnings (year } t)}{\text{Index of male manual weekly earnings (year 1975)}}$$

and w_t^* and y_t^* were the variables used in predicting backwards the probabilities of participation.

The cohort effects are obtained from Tables 13 and 15 in Joshi *et al.* (1981), evaluated at the mean of the variables included in their equation (1) of Table 13. Rather than using these effects directly we estimated them from a fitted line to avoid the sudden lack in trend that those effects have for generations born after 1935. Then we multiplied the predicted probability of participation of each woman by the estimated cohort effect corresponding to the year of her birth. After doing this we compared the predicted participation rate in 1975 with the actual participation rate in that year, and we adjusted the cohort effects by a common factor to make both rates equal. This adjusted cohort effect was then the one used in the analysis. Formally, let P_i be the probability of participation

120

Table A5.1. Index of real manual earnings. Base 1930 = 100

Year	Real female manual hourly earnings	Real male manual weekly earnings
1931	106.9	107.2
1932	106.7	107.5
1933	106.7	107.8
1934	108.1	108.8
1935	108.2	108.3
1936	108.3	109.0
1937	104.8	106.1
1938	109.6	110.3
1939	118.1	123.7
1940	113.6	122.9
1941	117.8	126.1
1942	136.6	121.9
1943	142.3	138.9
1944	148.2	139.8
1945	144.7	131.6
1946	147.0	126.6
1947	152.3	127.4
1948	152.5	128.5
1949	156.4	129.0
1950	157.5	131.8
1951	159.5	133.2
1952	155.2	131.2
1953	159.8	134.8
1954	165.9	143.1
1955	170.0	149.3
1956	174.1	151.8
1957	178.2	154.8
1958	178.4	153.4
1959	184.8	161.1
1960	197.2	171.0
1961	202.4	174.4
1962	203.7	173.1
1963	207.3	179.1
1964	215.1	188.4
1965	224.0	193.5
1966	229.8	193.1
1967	234.6	198.6

Table A5.1. (continued)

Year	Real female manual hourly earnings	Real male manual weekly earnings
1968	239.2	204.0
1969	244.6	208.8
1970	267.0	221.9
1971	277.1	223.6
1972	298.0	241.8
1973	316.9	252.8
1974	352.1	259.0
1975	362.4	255.5

Source: Halsey, British Labour Statistics, Historical Abstract, *New Earnings Survey*.

of the ith woman in 1975, and c_i the cohort effect corresponding to her year of birth. The first step consisted in defining for each woman in the sample

$$P_i' = c_i P_i$$

Then we compared the predicted participation rate

$$\left[\sum_{i=1}^{N} P_i' \right] / N$$

where N is the total number of women in the sample (participants and non-participants), with the actual participation rate

$$\left[\sum_{i=1}^{N} P_i \right] / N$$

and defined the factor of adjustment ϕ as

$$\phi = \left[\sum_{i=1}^{N} P_i \right] \Big/ \left[\sum_{i=1}^{N} P_i' \right]$$

which is equal to 1.096. Then the adjusted cohort effect used in the analysis is

$$c_i^* = \phi c_i$$

so that, for all periods of time, the probability of each woman was predicted as

$$P_{it}^* = c_i^* P_{it}, \quad \text{for all } t$$

This ensures both that participation probabilities are corrected for fixed

Table A5.2. Cohort effects

Year of birth	Cohort effect
1916	0.884
1917	0.890
1918	0.896
1919	0.902
1920	0.907
1921	0.913
1922	0.919
1923	0.925
1924	0.930
1925	0.936
1926	0.942
1927	0.948
1928	0.953
1929	0.959
1930	0.965
1931	0.971
1932	0.976
1933	0.982
1934	0.988
1935	0.994
1936	0.999
1937	1.005
1938	1.011
1939	1.017
1940	1.022
1941	1.028
1942	1.034
1943	1.040
1944	1.045
1945	1.051
1946	1.057
1947	1.063
1948	1.068
1949	1.074
1950	1.080
1951	1.086
1952	1.092

Table A5.2. (continued)

Year of birth	Cohort effect
1953	1.097
1954	1.103
1955	1.109
1956	1.115
1957	1.120
1958	1.126

Source: Joshi *et al.*

Table A5.3. Equation (5.5)

Variable	Coefficient	Standard error
Other family income (log)	0.535	0.075
Wife's wage (log)	− 0.210	0.131
Constant	− 2.904	1.911
Number of children aged		
0−2	1.218	0.062
3−5	0.659	0.049
6−10	0.097	0.036
11−13	− 0.017	0.050
14−15	0.043	0.063
15−17	− 0.152	0.104
18 and over	0.099	0.188
Age		
Under 25	− 0.051	0.094
25−34	− 0.093	0.069
45−54	0.206	0.069
55−59	0.658	0.093
Ethnic group		
Coloured, West Indians	− 0.365	0.257
Other coloured	0.182	0.232
Irish born	0.052	0.136
Long-standing illness	0.218	0.054
Number of observations	3938	
Log-likelihood	− 2255	

Note: This equation is estimated using the 'Probit' method.

cohort differences and that the adjusted probabilities predict correctly the participation rate for the period in which the model was estimated. The adjusted cohort effects (c_i^*) are presented in Table A5.2.

Tables A5.3 to A5.7 present the estimates of the auxiliary labour supply model used to predict backward the probabilities of participation.

Table A5.4. Equation (5.6)

Variable	Coefficient	Standard error
Constant	− 0.271	0.039
Education leaving age		
15	0.052	0.025
16	0.155	0.030
17	0.228	0.040
18	0.246	0.055
19+	0.632	0.035
Father's occupation		
Professional and managerial	0.054	0.039
Other manual	0.051	0.042
Skilled	− 0.014	0.033
Semi-skilled	− 0.053	0.035
Non-professional self-employed	0.008	0.045
Other	− 0.019	0.058
Age		
Under 25	− 0.029	0.029
25−34	− 0.009	0.023
45−54	0.045	0.025
55−59	0.014	0.039
Ethnic group		
Coloured, West Indian	− 0.086	0.084
Other coloured	0.188	0.093
Irish born	0.058	0.053
Long-standing illness	− 0.058	0.021
λ	− 0.042	0.031
$\bar{R}^2$	0.173	
N	2331	

Note: This equation was also corrected for selectivity bias but, as the coefficient on λ indicates, this first-round correction was not significant.

Table A5.5. Equation (5.9)

Variable	Coefficient	Standard error
Constant	3.651	0.067
Age	0.028	0.003
Age squared	− 0.0004	0.00004
Secondary education (0, 1 Dummy)	− 0.767	0.216
Higher education (0, 1 Dummy)	− 1.137	0.193
Age × secondary education dummy	0.036	0.011
Age × higher education dummy	0.055	0.010
Age squared × secondary education dummy	− 0.0003	0.0001
Age squared × higher education dummy	− 0.0005	0.0001
Occupation		
Manager (large establishment)	0.056	0.023
Manager (small establishment)	− 0.163	0.027
Non-manual (intermediate)	− 0.257	0.024
Non-manual (junior)	− 0.347	0.023
Manual (supervisory)	− 0.243	0.025
Manual (skilled)	− 0.307	0.021
Manual (semi-skilled)	− 0.393	0.022
Personal service worker	− 0.452	0.066
Manual (unskilled)	− 0.398	0.033
Armed forces	− 0.261	0.044
$\bar{R}^2$	0.317	
N	3951	

Note: 'Primary education' is the omitted category in the set of education dummies, and 'Professional' the omitted category in the set of occupational dummies.

Table A5.6. Means and standard deviations of variables used in Tables A5.3, A5.4 and A5.5

Variable	Mean	Standard deviation
Participation	0.59	0.49
Other family income (£/week)	52.68	23.85
Wife's hourly earnings (£/h)	0.84	0.27
Number of children by age		
0−2	0.19	0.44
3−5	0.23	0.49
6−10	0.40	0.69
11−13	0.21	0.48
14−15	0.13	0.36
16−17	0.05	0.22
18 and over	0.01	0.11
Wife's age dummies		
Under 25	0.11	0.30
25−34	0.33	0.48
45−54	0.25	0.43
55−59	0.08	0.28
Wife's ethnic group		
Coloured, West Indian	0.007	0.056
Other coloured	0.009	0.099
Irish born	0.03	0.16
Wife's long-standing illness	0.21	0.40
Wife's education leaving age		
15	0.37	0.48
16	0.13	0.34
17	0.06	0.23
18	0.03	0.16
19+	0.08	0.27
Wife's father's occupation		
Professional and managerial	0.12	0.33
Other manual	0.09	0.29
Skilled	0.41	0.49
Semi-skilled	0.21	0.41
Non-professional self-employed	0.07	0.25
Other	0.03	0.16
Husband's age	40.41	11.46
Husband's age squared	1764.28	959.30
Husband's secondary education dummy	0.07	0.25
Husband's higher education dummy	0.11	0.31

Table A5.7. Coefficients and t-statistics for additional standardising variables used in Table 5.5

Independent variable	Men (1)	Women (2)	(3)	(4)
Non-white	− 0.086	0.010	0.008	0.014
	(2.195)	(0.177)	(0.132)	(0.243)
Long-standing illness	− 0.022	− 0.063	0.0004	− 0.011
	(1.777)	(3.260)	(0.019)	(0.581)
Occupation				
Manager (large	− 0.003	0.561	0.554	0.578
establishment)	(0.090)	(4.449)	(4.475)	(4.718)
Manager (small	− 0.227	0.078	0.059	0.106
establishment)	(6.727)	(0.602)	(0.465)	(0.840)
Non-manual	− 0.239	0.179	0.193	0.215
(intermediate)	(8.105)	(1.670)	(1.848)	(2.084)
Non-manual (junior)	− 0.488	− 0.043	− 0.020	0.023
	(16.820)	(0.393)	(0.184)	(0.214)
Manual (supervisory)	− 0.413	− 0.046	− 0.035	0.018
	(13.186)	(0.349)	(0.278)	(0.141)
Manual (skilled)	− 0.490	− 0.083	− 0.038	0.010
	(18.297)	(0.718)	(0.333)	(0.091)
Manual (semi-skilled)	− 0.564	− 0.136	− 0.107	− 0.064
	(19.821)	(1.216)	(0.977)	(0.588)
Personal service worker	− 0.707	− 0.139	− 0.096	− 0.052
	(8.874)	(1.247)	(0.884)	(0.483)
Manual (unskilled)	− 0.574	− 0.179	− 0.127	− 0.093
	(14.114)	(1.602)	(1.160)	(0.862)
Armed forces	− 0.377	−	−	−
	(6.605)			
Industry				
Agriculture	− 0.358	− 0.242	− 0.251	− 0.245
	(5.562)	(2.219)	(2.345)	(2.319)
Mining	0.023	0.093	0.079	0.103
	(0.479)	(0.347)	(0.303)	(0.399)
Food	− 0.901	0.043	0.047	0.050
	(1.850)	(0.545)	(0.587)	(0.635)
Coal and oil	0.116	0.333	0.281	0.306
	(1.348)	(1.244)	(1.078)	(1.188)
Chemicals	− 0.012	0.089	0.098	0.109
	(0.240)	(0.995)	(1.114)	(1.260)
Metals	− 0.037	0.073	0.060	0.075
	(0.774)	(0.697)	(0.588)	(0.743)

Table A5.7. (continued)

Independent variable	Men	Women		
	(1)	(2)	(3)	(4)
Engineering	− 0.025	0.077	0.081	0.081
	(0.593)	(1.084)	(1.159)	(1.177)
Instruments	− 0.111	0.155	0.163	0.140
	(1.547)	(1.281)	(1.381)	(1.197)
Shipbuilding	− 0.074	0.168	0.062	0.068
	(1.364)	(1.023)	(0.361)	(0.396)
Textiles	− 0.137	− 0.048	− 0.046	− 0.037
	(2.551)	(0.571)	(0.563)	(0.642)
Leather	− 0.175	− 0.038	− 0.015	− 0.018
	(1.599)	(0.248)	(0.105)	(0.122)
Clothing	− 0.155	− 0.026	− 0.012	0.0012
	(1.510)	(0.342)	(0.164)	(0.016)
Bricks, etc.	− 0.069	0.154	0.152	0.143
	(1.351)	(1.634)	(1.647)	(1.562)
Timber	− 0.052	− 0.089	− 0.106	− 0.107
	(0.820)	(0.687)	(0.840)	(0.857)
Paper	− 0.006	− 0.032	− 0.035	− 0.036
	(0.111)	(0.375)	(0.315)	(0.424)
Construction	− 0.086	− 0.007	− 0.032	− 0.035
	(2.012)	(0.064)	(0.315)	(0.345)
Utilities	− 0.033	0.194	0.163	0.182
	(0.648)	(1.827)	(1.544)	(1.739)
Transport	− 0.097	0.115	0.107	0.110
	(2.232)	(1.436)	(1.349)	(1.405)
Distribution	− 0.165	− 0.155	− 0.125	− 0.177
	(3.724)	(2.207)	(1.811)	(1.076)
Finance	0.058	0.108	0.108	0.110
	(1.204)	(1.423)	(1.444)	(1.489)
Professional and scientific	− 0.059	0.023	0.058	0.069
	(1.273)	(0.331)	(0.825)	(0.999)
Miscellaneous services	− 0.225	− 0.118	− 0.080	− 0.081
	(4.716)	(1.654)	(1.132)	(1.157)
Public administration and defence	− 0.081	0.168	0.160	0.163
	(1.786)	(2.230)	(2.167)	(2.231)

Note: The omitted category in the set of occupational dummies is 'Professional' whereas in the set of industrial dummies 'Other manufacturing' is the excluded one.

Notes

1 An excellent survey of the empirical evidence on sex discrimination and on the impact of anti-discrimination legislation in the US can be found in Blau (1983).

2 In Chapter 2 we consider the evolution for the last ten years of relative pay in part-time work only, and the temporal pattern detected is very similar to that in Chart 1.1.

3 In this summary we are using the average of two estimates shown in Table 5.6 of Chapter 5. The first is obtained when differences in the occupational and industrial structure of male and female employment are not taken into account, and the second when they are taken into account. The 15 per cent figure given in the text is the average of the 2.7 and 28.1 per cent figures given in Table 5.6.

4 These figures refer to a comparison between men's salaries and the salaries of women who *are* participating in the labour force. If the comparison were made between men's salaries and the potential salaries of all women, participant and non-participant, the corresponding figures would be 21 per cent due to differences in attributes, 63 per cent due to non-participation and 16 per cent of unexplained residual.

5 The extent of success of the legislation would still be higher if the measurement of the potential gap was not made conditional on the decision to participate. The corresponding figures in this case would be 30 per cent if we assume that all the differential explained by non-participation is discriminatory, and 71 per cent if we assume that it is not.

6 The same conclusions follow when we look at all women (part-time and full-time, relative to full-time men). The corresponding information for these aggregated data is presented in Table A2.1 and Charts A2.1 A2.2 and A2.3 in the Annex to this Chapter.

7 This aspect, of course, could only be captured fully if sectors were defined in terms of homogeneous jobs. The industrial or occupational divisions, although they go some way towards standardising for differences in job characteristics, are still too broad.

8 The full expression is

$$\dot{r} = \sum_{i=1}^{n} k_i \dot{f}_i + \sum_{i=1}^{n} k_i \dot{r}_i + \sum_{i=1}^{n} k_i \dot{s}_i + \sum_{i=1}^{n} k_i \dot{f}_i \dot{r}_i$$

$$+ \sum_{i=1}^{n} k_i \dot{f}_i \dot{s}_i + \sum_{i=1}^{n} k_i \dot{r}_i \dot{s}_i + \sum_{i=1}^{n} k_i \dot{f}_i \dot{r}_i \dot{s}_i$$

9 For 17 industries, employing 95% of the female manual labour force, the 1970–80 change in relative (female/male) wages (i.e. $\dot{r}$) was +17.9%, $\Sigma k \dot{f}_i$ was − 0.7%, $\Sigma k_i \dot{r}_i$ was +18.4% and $\Sigma k_i \dot{s}_i$ was − 0.4%. (These estimates are in line with those of Table 2.5.) See Tables A2.2, A2.3 and A2.4 in the Annex for data on relative hourly earnings by industry (manual and non-manual) and occupation.

10 It is difficult to say anything about changes in the quality of labour on the basis of the *New Earnings Survey*, since this source does not provide any information on the level of education of workers included in the sample.

11 In 1973, 67 per cent of full-time women and 75 per cent of full-time men were covered by a collective agreement or wages board.

12 It should be noted that the rate figures in Table 3.1 are indexed to be 100 in 1976. The actual ratio of average female rates over average male rates will differ from 1, even after full equality is achieved, due to differences in the distributions of male and female employment.

13 The higher increase of relative earnings in the covered sector is explained by the fact that in this sector the relative position of men deteriorated still more than that of women (a fall of 2.9 per cent).

14 Discrimination tastes by male employees would, in the long run, lead to complete segregation rather than to wage differentials. Also Arrow (1972) has noted that in a world without adjustment costs, even employer discrimination would not be able to generate discriminatory wage differentials. If adjustment costs are important, however, the wage differentials generated by discriminatory practices may be difficult to wipe out, even in the long run.

15 See Landes (1968) for a detailed analysis of the effects of anti-discriminatory legislation along these lines.

16 The equal pay legislation may have also influenced the stability of female employment. An attempt to evaluate this issue can be found in Tzannatos and Zabalza (1985). Although the evidence is not completely clear, the exercise suggests that the variability of female employment may have been reduced as a result of both the Equal Pay and the Sex Discrimination Acts. However, this effect is largely concentrated on non-manual workers in non-manufacturing, who were already enjoying a relatively high degree of employment stability.

17 Because of this we will only use 'single equation' methods of estimation. However, in the theoretical discussion that follows we consider explicitly both demand and supply.

18 This assumes that the situation before the implementation of the anti-discriminatory legislation was one of equilibrium, with relative wages being determined by both demand and supply.

19 The form of these fixed weights is suggested by the following considerations. Let the production function in sector i be

$$Q_i = R_i M_i^{\alpha_i} F_i^{\beta_i} \qquad\qquad (a)$$

where R stands for all other factors entering production, Q is output and α and β parameters. In equilibrium, each sector's relative demand will be

$$\frac{F_i}{M_i} = A_i \frac{W_m}{W_f} \qquad\qquad (b)$$

where $A_i = \beta_i/\alpha_i$. Aggregating this demand function for the whole economy, we obtain

$$\frac{F}{M} = \frac{W_m}{W_f} \left(\Sigma A_i \frac{M_i}{M}\right) \qquad\qquad (c)$$

which suggests that, in addition to relative wages, total relative demand will also depend on the industrial structure, represented here by the expression within parentheses. Then the weights A_i in (c) can be estimated using (b) as $A_i = (F_i W_f / M_i W_m)$, which is precisely what we do in the text.

20 See also Wachter (1970) for an empirical analysis, based on US data, of the movements of relative wage differentials over the cycle.

21 In the context of a supply relationship, Joshi *et al.* (1981) also find that an index of education is highly correlated with time and that this makes it difficult to isolate its separate effect.

22 See Joshi *et al.* (1981) for empirical evidence on the effect of fertility on female participation over time.

23 Given the semi-logarithmic specification used, the effect of the dummy coefficients is

$$\frac{(W_f/W_m)'}{(W_f/W_m)} = \exp(\Sigma \text{ dummy coefficients})$$

where (W_f/W_m) and $(W_f/W_m)'$ are the rates of earnings before and after the legislation respectively.

24 That is, according to this model, points A and C both belong to the supply relationship, but in the plane $\ln(W_f/W_m)/\ln(F/M)$ this function may have had a slope steeper than the broken line in Figure 4.1 and shifted rightwards during the period considered, or it may have had a flatter slope and shifted leftwards.

25 The logarithm of the relative wage could also be decomposed in the following manner

$$\ln(W_m) - \ln(W_f) = \beta(X_m - X_f) + X_m(\alpha - \beta) \qquad (5.3')$$

where the two components have the same interpretation as those in (5.3), but where the base of reference is now different. The existence of this second possibility is due to the 'index number' nature of this decomposition. In general $(5.3')$ gives a slightly different partition, and authors sometimes resolve the problem by offering both (or some average of both) alternatives.

26 If experience was defined more narrowly in terms of, say, the number of hours worked in the past, the endogeneity problem may be a significant one also for men.

27 See Bloom and Killingsworth (1982) for a discussion of this bias in discrimination studies and for a survey of the literature.

28 Education is another variable with some claims to endogeneity. In our context however this does not represent much of a problem since what we are interested in is the prediction of market experience *after* school is completed. Education can therefore be treated as predetermined.

29 We are indebted to H. Joshi for pointing out this problem and for suggesting the use of the cohort effects estimated in Joshi *et al.* (1981).

30 Equation (2) of Table 5.4 should not be taken as representative of the work done by other authors in this area, but as a benchmark over which to evaluate the influence of our methodology. Previous authors (see, for instance, Greenhalgh (1980)) have of course been aware of the effect that time spent out of the labour force may have on female wages, and have tried to control for this by including variables such as the number of children and their age. The method proposed here can be interpreted as a more structural way of dealing with this problem, which permits a more direct identification of the effect of actual experience and home time on wages.

31 The GHS data on which the equations of Table 5.4 have been estimated only provide data on children presently at home. Thus for older families the effect of family composition on participation may have been underestimated since we may have ignored children no longer living with their parents. To see the extent of this problem, we repeated the estimation in Table 5.4 for families in which the wife was less than 40 years old, and found the same qualitative results, with the coefficient on actual experience rising and becoming significant, and that on home time being negative and significant. The absolute effects were somewhat higher than those in Table 5.4, as we would expect from this younger and better educated subsample.

32 This is the method generally followed by previous sex discrimination studies based on British data. See Greenhalgh (1980) and Siebert and Sloane (1981).

33 Note that in evaluating the wage differential with the comparison
    (1) — (4) the variable λ does not play any direct role. What we want
    in this case is to compare the male wage with the overall expected
    female wage (that is, with the wage structure relevant to both parti-
    cipants and non-participants). This expected wage $E(w)$ is equal to
    the conditional wage for participants times the probability of parti-
    cipation plus the conditional wage for non-participants times the
    probability of non-participation. Using the Heckman (1979) model,
    it is easy to show (see, for instance, Maddala (1983), p. 367) that
    this expected wage is

$$E(w) = (\beta X_f + \eta\lambda)(1 - F(Z)) + (\beta X_f + \eta\bar{\lambda})F(Z)$$

where η is the regression coefficient of the variable λ, λ is defined
as in expression (5.11), $\lambda = f(Z)/(1 - F(Z))$ and $\bar{\lambda} = -f(Z)/F(Z)$.
Substituting these expressions into the above expectation we find

$$E(w) = \left(\beta X_f + \eta\frac{f(Z)}{1 - F(Z)}\right)(1 - F(Z) + \left(\beta X_f - \eta\frac{f(Z)}{F(Z)}\right)F(Z)$$

or

$$E(w) = \beta X_f$$

where the variable λ does not appear. Therefore the partition obtained with the comparison (1) — (4) in Table 5.6 is different from
that obtained with the comparison (1) — (3) due only to the new
coefficients which are estimated when the wage equation is corrected
for selectivity.

34 Since the correction for selective bias gives us the female wage equa-
    tion relevant to both participants and non-participants, the residual
    percentage attributable to discrimination should be evaluated using
    the unconditional means for the whole female population. In Table
    5.6, the comparison (1) — (4) uses means only for participants,
    because there is no data on the industrial distribution of non-partici-
    pants. The bias involved, however, is small. If we restrict the com-
    parison to the small specification, then the unconditional mean
    values can be used. These give a percentage attributable to discrimi-
    nation of 16.2, which is close to the 19.2 figure obtained with the
    conditional means. The results are also very similar for the other
    two differentials. Using the unconditional means we obtained 13.9
    per cent due to differences in attributes and 69.9 per cent due to
    depreciation, which are quite close to the figures 11.1 and 69.7
    shown in the third row of Table 5.6.

References

Aigner, D.J. and Cain, G.G. (1977), Statistical theories of discrimination in the labor market, *Industrial and Labour Relations Review*, pp. 175–87.

Arrow, K.J. (1972), Models of job discrimination, in *Racial Discrimination in Economic Life*, A.H. Pascal (ed), Lexington Books, D.C. Heath, Mass.

Ashenfelter, O. (1970), Changes in labor market discrimination over time, *Journal of Human Resources*, Vol. 5, pp. 403–29.

Ashenfelter, O. and Layard, R. (1979), The effects of income policies upon differentials, London School of Economics, Centre for Labour Economics Discussion Paper No. 44.

Becker, G.S. (1964), *Human Capital: A Theoretical and Empirical Analysis, with Special Reference to Education*, National Bureau of Economic Research, Columbia University Press, New York.

Becker, G.S. (1971), *The Economics of Discrimination*, 2nd ed., University of Chicago Press, Chicago.

Blau, F.D. (1983), Discrimination against women: theory and evidence, Mimeo, University of Illinois at Urbana-Champaign. Forthcoming in *Labor Economics: Modern Views*, W.A. Darity (ed), Martinus Nijhoff, Boston.

Blinder, A.S. (1973), Wage discrimination: reduced form and structural estimates, *Journal of Human Resources*, Vol. 8, pp. 436–55.

Blinder, A.S. (1976), On dogmatism in human capital theory, *Journal of Human Resources*, Vol. 11, pp. 8–22.

Bloom, D.E. and Killingsworth, M.R. (1982), Pay discrimination research and litigation: the use of regression, *Industrial Relations*, Vol. 21.

Butler, R. and Heckman, J.J. (1977), The government's impact on the labour market status of black Americans, in *Equal Rights and Industrial Relations*, J.S. Hausman *et al.* (eds), Industrial Relations Research Association Series, University of Wisconsin.

Chiplin, B., Curran, M.M. and Parsley, C.J. (1980), Relative female earnings in Great Britain and the impact of legislation, in *Women and Low Pay*, P.J. Sloane (ed), Macmillan, London.

Freeman, R.B. (1973), Changes in the labour market for black Americans, *Brookings Papers on Economic Activity*, Vol. 1, pp. 67–120.

Greenhalgh, C. (1980), Male–female wage differentials in Great Britain: is marriage an equal opportunity?, *Economic Journal*, Vol. 90, pp. 751–75.

Gregory, M.B. and Thomson, A.W.J. (1981). The coverage mark-up, bargaining structure and earnings in Britain, 1973 and 1978, *British Journal of Industrial Relations*, Vol. 19, pp. 26–37.

Hausman, J.A. (1978), Specification tests in econometrics, *Econometrica*, Vol. 46, pp. 1251–71.

Heckman, J. (1977), Sample selection bias as a specification error with an application to the estimation of labour supply functions, National Bureau of Economic Research, Working Paper No. 172.

Heckman, J. (1979), Sample selection bias as a specification error, *Econometrica*, Vol. 47, pp. 153–61.

Hepple, B.A. (1984). *Equal Pay and the Industrial Tribunals*, Sweet and Maxwell, London.

Joshi, H., Layard, R. and Owen, S. (1981), Female labour supply in post-war Britain: a cohort approach, London School of Economics, Centre for Labour Economics, Discussion Paper No. 79.

Landes, W.M. (1968), The economics of fair employment laws, *Journal of Political Economy*, Vol. 76, pp. 507–52.

Maddala, G.S. (1983), *Limited-Dependent and Qualitative Variables in Econometrics*, Cambridge University Press, Cambridge.

Malkiel, B.G. and Malkiel, J.A. (1973), Male–female pay differentials in professional employment, *American Economic Review*, Vol. 63, pp. 693–705.

Mincer, J. (1966), Labour force participation and unemployment: a review of recent evidence, in *Prosperity and Unemployment*, R.A. Gordon and M.S. Gordon (eds), John Wiley, New York.

Mincer, J. (1974), *Schooling, Experience and Earnings*, Columbia University Press, New York.

Mincer, J. and Polachek, S. (1974), Family investments in human capital: earnings of women, *Journal of Political Economy*, Vol. 82, pp. S.76–S.108.

Mincer, J. and Polachek, S. (1978), Women's earnings re-examined, *Journal of Human Resources*, Vol. 13, pp. 118–34.

Oxaca, R. (1973), Male–female wage differentials in urban labour markets, *International Economic Review*, Vol. 14, pp. 693–709.

Phelps, E.S. (1972), The statistical theory of racism and sexism, *American Economic Review*, Vol. 62, pp. 659–61.

Siebert, W.S. and Sloane, P.J. (1981), The measurement of sex and marital status discrimination at the workplace, *Economica*, Vol. 48, pp. 125–41.

Snell, M.W., Glucklich, P. and Povall, M. (1981), *Equal Pay and Opportunities*, Research Paper No. 20, Department of Employment, London.

Stewart, M.B. and Greenhalgh, C.A. (1982), Work history patterns and the occupational attainment of women, Warwick Economic Research Paper No. 12, University of Warwick.

Tzannatos, Z. and Zabalza, A. (1985), The effect of sex anti-discriminatory legislation on the variability of female employment, *Applied Economics* (forthcoming).

Wachter, M.L. (1970), Cyclical variation in the interindustry wage structure, *American Economic Review*, Vol. 60, pp. 75–84.

Zabalza, A. (1983), The CES utility function, non-linear budget constraints and labour supply. Results on female participation and hours, *Economic Journal*, Vol. 93, pp. 312–30.

Zabalza, A. and Tzannatos, Z. (1982), The effect of Equal Pay legislation on the variability of female employment, London School of Economics, Centre for Labour Economics, Working Paper No. 407.

Author index

Subject index

age
  decomposition of changes in pay by, 30–2
agreements, collective, 1, 7–9
  changes in coverage, 113–4
  coverage, 37, 38, 131n
  decomposition of changes in pay by, 42–46
  manual workers, 38–40

cohort, effects of, 79, 120, 125

decomposition of average pay changes
  formula, 23, 25, 131n
  by age, 30–2
  by agreements, 42–3
  by industries, 26–8
  by occupation, 28–30
discrimination
  measurement of, 12, 70, 73
  outstanding, 14–15, 88–94
  tastes, theory of, 50–51, 131n

elasticity of relative demand
  aggregate, 58
  private sector, 65
employment
  aggregate, 3–5, 18–21
  full-time, 17–18
  manual, 17, 18, 36
  non-manual, 17, 18, 36
  by occupations, 22–4, 30
  part-time, 4, 19–20
  private sector, 5–6
Equal Pay Act
  amendment, 103–5
  description of, 97–102
  timing, 10–11, 38, 56

experience
  actual v. potential, 12–3, 73–6
  effect on wages, 85–8

fertility, 57

Hausman test, 66

incomes policies, 1, 9, 17–18, 49, 56–7, 60, 68
index of industrial employment, 55, 132n

manual workers, *see* employment; pay

non-compliance, penalties of, 10, 52
non-labour income, 57
non-manual workers, *see* employment; pay
non-participation, effects of, 2, 13–4, 71, 92–4

participation, probability of, 75–6
pay
  average, 2–3, 16–18
  distribution of, 33–4
  full-time, 17, 33, 38, 40
  manual, 17, 33, 38, 40
  non-manual, 17, 33, 40
  part-time, 20
  private sector, 11
  public sector, 18
  of teachers, 43
private sector
  effects of EPA, 62–5
  employment, 5–6
  pay, 7, 11, 28